HELLO MUM, I'M OKAY BUT...

Terri Inskip

ISBN 978-1-8381059-1-4
Also available as an e-book

Book design by The Art of Communication   www.book-design.co.uk
First published in the UK 2020

Dedication

To my wonderful husband,
children and grandchildren

Contents

Epigraph

There is no such word as 'can't'

Disclaimer

Some names have been changed in order to protect
the privacy of individuals

PREFACE

The smell of mustiness hit me when I dug out the old ships' logs stored in a trunk in the attic. As I read through them once again, all sense of time was lost whilst I relived those wonderful adventures I had on the high seas. Back in the sixties and seventies everything was so basic. Satellite navigation was unheard of and the sextant was the most precious thing on board, followed closely by our gimbal Rolex timer and direction finder. It was after I received the logs that I promised myself I would write down all that I could remember of my adventures. Over forty years later, I finally managed to do it. It took coming down with a mystery illness during the summer of 2019 to jolt me into action. Unable to continue my usual active life, it gave me the opportunity to sit down and put pen to paper, or to be more exact, tap away on my laptop. It kept me sane. I am pleased to say I am now fully recovered and back to enjoying life to the full.

The initial purpose was to provide my kids and grandkids with some detail of my past, and if nothing else, it would help them put together some sort of eulogy when the time came. Blimey, how morbid is that! But hey, that was what the illness was doing to me at the time. It was a bit of a wake-up call. Before I knew what I was doing, my notes had developed into a manuscript, and it wasn't long before I realised that if I included my whole life to date, it would be far too long. So, this book covers my adventures up to when I decided to return to UK and start on some sort of career. That was back in 1977. As it turned out, I ended up having a number of different and interesting, sometimes challenging, careers with a few personal happenings thrown in. I feel another book coming on ...

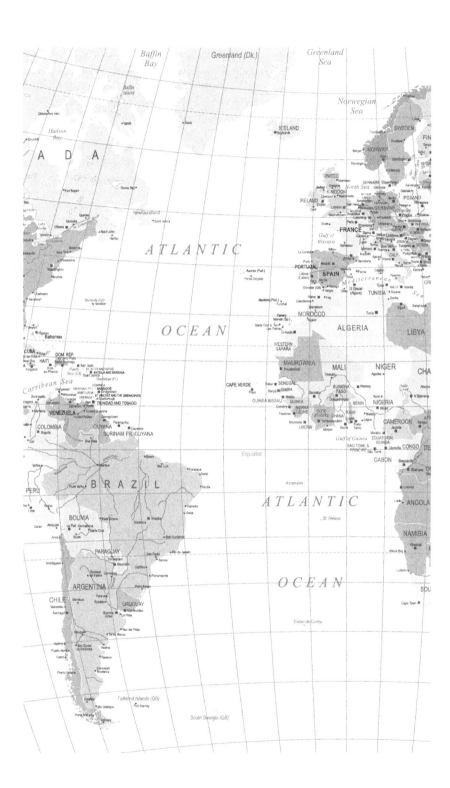

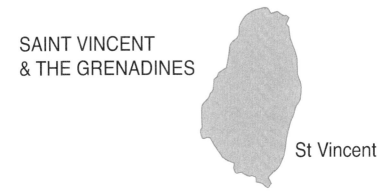

SAINT VINCENT
& THE GRENADINES

St Vincent

Bequia

Battowia
Baliceaux

Carribean Sea

Mustique

Canouan

Mayreau Tobago Cays

Union
Island

Palm Island

Petit St Vincent

Carriacou

GRENADA

Chapter 1 - Essex Girl

No matter how many times I took in the view, I still found it breathtaking. I was sipping a freshly squeezed lime squash, enjoying the cooling trade winds. It was February 1971 and I was at Freddy and Sue Harris's house on the island of St Vincent in the Grenadines, part of the Windward Islands in the West Indies. The house was on a cliff top. Where the lush green lawn ended, the ocean began. The water went from the palest of turquoise gradually deepening to a deep velvet blue. You could clearly see the islands of Battowia and Baliceaux ahead, with the larger island of Bequia to the right, and further away you could just about make out the outline of Mustique.

But at this moment the view became a blur whilst I sat reflecting on my life, all twenty-two years of it. I guess this must often happen to people when they experience some sort of trauma or accident, and this had certainly happened to me. It was like hitting the rewind button back to my first memories and then pressing the play button.

⋙⋘

I was born at home in Dagenham, Essex, in 1948, on what was then, and maybe still is, the largest council estate in Europe. I was named Teresa Audrey Sylvia Pegg. Audrey was my mum's name and Sylvia was her sister's name, who was also my godmother. As I discovered over the years, having two middle names is a right pain when filling in forms. My mum insisted including Sylvia as she didn't want my initials to be TAP – I never did understand the logic or the importance of this.

My parents first met at the local cycling club when they were still at school. They were married in the spring of 1946, Mum being nineteen and Dad twenty-two. That is young by today's standards, but, like so many back then, surviving World War Two matured them way beyond their years. Soon after they met, war broke out. An order was issued that all children in their area must be evacuated. This included Mum, then aged fourteen, her younger sister, Iris, and her brother, Reg, who was only six. Being sixteen, her older sister Sylvia was allowed to remain. It must be been heart-wrenching for my grandparents to have to wave goodbye to their three children not knowing where they were going, whether they would be properly looked after and if they would ever see them again. In desperation, my nan purposely packed my uncle Reg's possessions in the same suitcase as my mum's, with the hope they would not be separated. They ended up in Norfolk with a very unkind lady who was more interested in making them go regularly to Baptist church than trying to make their lives a little happier. It was a while before my nan could visit them, and as soon as she realised the situation she had them moved to a loving family who remained everlasting dear friends, especially to my uncle Reg.

Once Mum reached fifteen she was allowed to return home. Being a tailoress by trade, my nan had taught all three daughters how to sew, so Mum worked as a machinist in a clothing factory, mostly making military uniforms. This meant commuting by train to Tottenham Court Road in London. Already the night-time London Blitz had begun. Mum endured and survived the awful eleven weeks, sometimes witnessing horrific scenes en route and often having to walk part of the way due to track damage. Sometimes a raid would have already started by the time she arrived back at Beacontree Station. Instead of seeking shelter, she would run down the hill and head home where her mum would be waiting at the front door with sandwiches, a flask of tea and blankets. Together they would run through the house and down to the Anderson shelter at the bottom of the garden. By then, her older sister Sylvia had joined the RAF. As our end of the estate wasn't too close to the docks, I don't believe any bombs were dropped there. The biggest hazard for Mum was getting hit by shrapnel from the dogfighting going on overhead.

As soon as Dad was able to, he joined the Royal Navy as a gunner. He served on quite a few ships but spent a good part of the time in the North Atlantic with the Russian convoys. He witnessed many a ship being torpedoed and on one occasion, whilst in pursuit of the enemy, saw his own ship plough through survivors struggling in the sea. He also served on HMS Bulldog and witnessed the capture of the Enigma machine and code books from the German submarine U-110. At the time no one knew how significant this was, and little did they know how much it would change the course of the war. The crew did know something important had happened, though, as once they arrived in Faslane in Scotland all leave was cancelled. Dad also spent time in the Far East, where they brought back some of the pitiful survivors from the prison camps. Only in his later years did he talk about his experiences during the war. He said he would never forget the look in the eyes of those survivors. I shall never forget the tears running down his face.

My mum and dad had a wonderful and happy marriage which lasted for just under sixty years until my dad died of cancer. They were true soulmates. Two years after they were married I came along, and then my sister Janet arrived two years later. My claim to fame in my first year was that I got to eat the first banana that arrived in our street after the war ended. It was decided that the youngest child in our road should have it, and that was me. I had my own ration book as food and items were still in short supply in 1948. One of my earliest memories, at the age of four and a half, was the Queen's coronation. Having sold their café, my nan and grandad bought a television with some of the money just before the event. As they were the only ones in the family to have one, we all went over to their house in Crow Lane to watch it and have a party. All the aunts and uncles came, and for us as a family it was a very special occasion and certainly one to celebrate.

Our playground was the streets, where we played all sorts of games including hopscotch and marbles using the drain covers. My sister and I, along with my best friend Jackie Goddard who lived just a few doors down, combined our winnings and ended up with a very large tin of marbles that included some prize sixers. We were good players. The hula hoop was also a big craze then, and we had a competition at our school to see who could last the longest – I was really chuffed when I came second. That was at Finnymore Road Primary, which later was renamed Godwin School. In the summer we would organise a sport's day, and that was when the mums would suddenly discover they had one or two fewer teaspoons, which we had pinched and tied with bows to give out as prizes.

As kids we stuck together and supported each other when there was trouble. I remember an Irish family in which the mum and dad often fought, sending their four kids flying out of the house in terror. This made me realise at quite a young age how fortunate I was that my own mum and dad were a very loving couple and rarely argued. Whilst living in Dagenham there was a polio outbreak which resulted in large queues of us kids waiting to be inoculated. Sadly, one of Dad's friend's daughter, Pat, was struck by the disease, which resulted in her being paralysed from the waist down for the rest of her life. We often used to visit the family and I remember feeling so very sorry for Pat, who was about my age.

Dad qualified as a carpenter once he completed his apprenticeship, which he had just started when war broke out. Mum worked from home doing peace work for a company, making stiff lace and boned petticoats in many colours, whilst busy raising us two kids. I thought they were so pretty and I often slipped one on, pretending to be a ballet dancer. I would sometimes help by turning out to the right side, using a blunt pencil, stitched-up strips of material that were made for the ties; a trick I have never forgotten. To begin with Mum had a Singer treadle sewing machine, and I used to squeeze under the table to sit and rock on the treadle. This was replaced with a new American Wilcox & Gibbs professional electric machine that folded into a walnut veneer cabinet. The motor made quite an alarming noise, and it never ceased to amaze me how incredibly fast my mum was able to run up seams on it. The fabric would just fly through the foot of the machine. This was in 1955 and it cost £60 which they paid by instalments. Mum was still using that machine at the age of eighty-five and now my sister Karen uses it.

There wasn't a lot of spare money but we never felt we missed out; and of course, thanks to Mum, we wore beautifully made dresses. When the Ford car works went on strike, which I seem to remember happened on a regular basis, there would be a door-to-door collection to help the families, and Mum and Dad would always put a shilling in the box. When I was eight, Dad had an accident at work. He fell off a roof and broke his back. No compensation was granted back then, so it must have been very tough financially although my sister and I were never made aware of this. For a time Dad slept on a put-you-up in the front room, and my sister Janet and I would rush home from school to sit and listen to one of Dad's stories. He used to make them up as he went along. They must have been good, as we would happily sit for ages listening to them, never getting bored. Gradually, his back improved enough for him to move around aided by a straightjacket to give him support. At this stage, before he went back to site work, Dad took a job selling ice cream. He had one of those pedal bikes with the cooler box on the front. As kids it was always exciting to see Dad arriving in our street, calling out 'Ice cream for sale'.

Our first few holidays were spent in the hop fields of Kent. I remember feeling very pleased with myself that I had filled one of the straw hop baskets all on my own, and whenever I smell hops it takes me straight back to those days. We travelled there in an open truck which we thought was great fun. The fathers joined us at the weekends. Later, once Mum and Dad managed to save up and buy a small car, we used to join forces with my Aunty Sylvia and Uncle Tom, and their two boys, Keith and Kevin, and go camping at a farm above Salcombe in Devon. We were quite jealous of our two cousins as they got to travel in a motorcycle and sidecar. Mum made the tent – a Canvas Bell type. I have such fond memories of those holidays. I can't ever remember it raining but I expect it did on occasion. Our favourite beach was in Sunny Cove, opposite Salcombe. There was, and still is, a small ferry boat that takes you to Mill Bay and from there we walked over the cliff to Sunny Cove. On one occasion I watched a group of young teenage boys and girls come ashore in sailing dinghies. I must have been about nine. The girls were wearing gorgeous, expensive-looking bikinis. I wasn't envious – just interested to see a different lifestyle. It must have made some impact on me as the memory is still very clear. I wonder if that planted the seed that started me not accepting my lot – or was it in the blood of this Dagenham girl?

When we were old enough we were allowed to go to Saturday morning pictures at the cinema at Heathway. My sister and I were given a shilling – 6d for getting in and 6d to spend. We would go on our roller skates and head straight to Woolworths to get our sweets before carrying on to the cinema. To begin with there would be a cartoon like Tom and Jerry, Woody Woodpecker or Bugs Bunny. Following this would be a serial like Batman, Lassie or Flash Gordon. Finally came the main feature film which often was cowboy or animal related. If we were lucky, we got to see one in colour. Going to Romford Market was a regular thing we used to do as a family on a Saturday afternoon. I absolutely loved the atmosphere and all the noise. There was always a lot of shouting from the fruit and veg stallholders, especially near the end of the day when they would drop their prices to get rid of what was left. That was one of the reasons why we went in the afternoons, so that Mum and Dad could pick up some bargains. There were plenty of material and haberdashery stalls as more women made their clothes back then. Mum and I would spend ages going through all the bales of fabric looking for just the right thing for a new dress or blouse. I absolutely loved going there near Christmas. All the stalls would be decked out in colourful tinsel and the air would be full of the smell of pine from the Christmas trees. And there would be so many toys for sale. As it got dark, all the fairy lights would come on, making the stalls look ever so pretty.

When I was eleven we moved to Chipping Ongar, which is in a more rural part of Essex. My parents managed to do a council house swap. When we were told we were going to move to Ongar I got very excited, thinking we were heading off to a tropical jungle. I think I got it confused with the Congo! We were still excited, though, at the thought of exchanging street play for running around in fields and woods. I went to the local secondary school, but I was a borderline case for grammar school. Two of us were interviewed for the one place available, and although I always fared better in classroom tests, the other girl was chosen. I wonder if it had anything to do with the fact that her father was a local councillor? Apparently, if it hadn't been for the age allowance, I would have made grammar school easily. Whenever I mention this age allowance issue I get blank looks, so I suspect it must have been a trial for a limited amount of time and maybe in only selected areas. Basically, the younger you were, the more marks were added to your eleven-plus results. Being born in September made me one of the eldest and therefore I received no extra marks. I believe there was an uproar about it at the time as it was seen to be very unfair. No matter when any of us were born during that year, we all started at the same time in September, which meant we all had the same amount of schooling up to when it was time to take the eleven-plus exams. Hey ho! As it turned out, Ongar Secondary School was one of the best in Essex, and I truly believe I was better off being in the top class of that school rather than struggle trying to compete with more intelligent minds in a grammar school; and it would have been a good forty-five-minute bus ride away instead of a ten-minute walk.

On the whole I enjoyed school, although I did struggle with English. Looking back, I believe I was a little dyslexic. My spelling was atrocious, and I tended to mess up big time on all theory work when taking exams. My love was mathematics and sport. I shall always remember Alf Jones, my maths teacher. He would patiently spend a lot of extra time going over various formulas with me. My problem was that I couldn't just accept and memorise them without fully understanding how and why each one was formed. He was such a dedicated teacher. And I had such a huge crush on the boys' PE teacher, Mr Gent. He was gorgeous, and when it was announced in assembly that he was engaged, I cried buckets. Netball in the winter and rounders in the summer were my two main sports, and by the time I was in the fourth form I was house captain and represented the school in both games. I played help shooter (now known as goal attack) in netball and first base in rounders. I was able to hit that rounders ball well hard, and being a left-hander it often went deep between first and second base, allowing me to score a rounder. I used to have to wait until the whole field moved round before I was bowled. We played well and were always near the top of the county leagues. Brentwood Grammar were our strongest opposition, especially in netball.

When I was thirteen I had a new baby sister. It wasn't planned and the pregnancy came as quite a surprise to Mum and Dad. They did try for another child for some years without luck. Dad had a bad attack of the measles as a young man, so they reckoned he had become infertile. Consequently, no precautions were taken. Mum, having had both myself and my sister Janet at home, really wanted this one in the local cottage hospital so she could get some peace and quiet. As there was no medical reason why she couldn't give birth at home, her request was refused. One day, on our way home from school, old Ma Short from two doors down grabbed me and Janet, gave us some tea and told us Mum was in labour. Dad finally came round when it was time for bed and took us back home. At that time the baby still hadn't arrived. I vividly remember lying in bed listening to Mum crying out in the room next door. I was convinced she was going to die and begged God not to let this happen. Dad got quite cross with me when I kept calling out, asking if Mum was all right. Eventually, Karen was born in the early hours of the morning and Dad brought her in to show us. I was so relieved when told Mum was okay and sleeping.

By the time I was fourteen I had a Saturday job in the

newspaper shop round the corner. I had been given my Aunty Mildred's old bicycle and wanted to save up and buy new bits for it. I loved that bike. I painted it light blue and brought new white mudguards, handle grips and a basket for the front. I had three gears put on it and replaced the hard saddle for a much bigger and springier one. My best friend Diane and I would cycle all over the place including Harlow new town, where we would have a swim in the Olympic-size glassed indoor pool and then cycle back. I also worked on Sundays at a posh pub up the road called The Stag, washing glasses. The hunt would meet there and part of my job was to take glasses of sherry out to them on a tray. Once I had dried the glasses out the back, I had to return them to the bar areas. The first room I would pass through was the tap room. The landlord showed me how to pour a pint and allowed me to serve the locals when it got busy in the saloon. It wasn't long before I became a fully fledged barmaid, and this was before I was fifteen! Mum knew but we daren't tell Dad, and of course the landlord was taking a big risk letting me do it. I loved it. When I had a big order of various drinks, the landlord would stand by and quietly check the amount I charged. I had to add up the cost of each drink in my head as I went along, often whilst talking to the customer. He was well impressed as I never got it wrong. I suppose that was the first time I realised I loved working in an environment where I could chat with people. It was around that time that I had my first boyfriend. We would go for long walks across the fields with a neighbour's dog. I can't recall the boyfriend's name now, but Mum wasn't impressed when I took him home as he had a dirty shirt collar. I remember proudly telling the girls at school that he kissed me sixteen times on one date.

The following year I was allowed to go to the school youth club but had to be home at 10.30 p.m. That was in 1963 – well into the Swinging Sixties. I was a mod but was still too young thankfully to get involved with all the clashes between the mods and rockers. One weekend a whole bunch of the older boys went off on their scooters down to Southend, and many got badly hurt in a nasty battle that hit the news. It was a really rebellious time for us teenagers. Once I got to the top of our road I would turn my skirt waistband up at least three times and apply more make-up – heavy mascara and very pale lipstick were the fashion. I managed to persuade Mum to buy me a pair of white knee-length boots which I wore to death. She was so angry when I purposely frayed the bottoms of my tweed flared trousers. I wore my hair short, backcombed with kiss curls at the side that I used to Sellotape in place each night. Jiving was still popular but individual dancing was becoming the thing. Often a group of us girls would jiggle away with our handbags in the middle whilst the boys watched on, deciding who they were going to try and chat up later.

I had a few different boyfriends over the following couple of years, but one boy stands out very clearly in my mind; and that was Neil Sharp. He had already left school but came to the youth club, as many did of his age. On our way back one night I realised I had forgotten my handbag. We shot back, thankfully retrieved it from behind the curtain on the windowsill, and headed back towards my house. As time was marching on, we parted at an alleyway at the top of my road so that Neil could leg it to catch the bus home. By then, after pacing up and down at home, Dad decided to come look for me. I was ten minutes late. He just happened to pass by the alleyway on the other side of the road as Neil and I were having a goodnight kiss. When he realised it was his daughter, he lost it. He shot across the road and gave Neil an almighty shove, sending him sprawling, and told him to bugger off. I flew down the road, and once home, went straight up to my room, sobbing and shouting that Dad had hurt my boyfriend. I could hear Mum having a go at my dad, telling him he shouldn't have done that. Once we had all calmed down, he came up to my room. Whilst cuddling me he apologised and tried to explain that it was due to the shock of seeing how grown up I had become. He suggested that Neil might like to come to tea the following Sunday so that he could apologise to him. I take my hat off to Neil, as he bravely accepted the invite. Years later when Dad walked into one of the local pubs, something he didn't often do, Neil was there and promptly brought Dad a drink, still called him Mr Pegg, and said that now he had children of his own, he fully understood Dad's actions all those years ago.

Chapter 2 – The Times They Are a-Changin'

In the sixties you could leave school at sixteen. About thirty of us opted to stay for an extra year to take the GCE O Level exams. I took the four maths papers, English literature, English language, domestic science and needlework. During this time I also learnt how to type and do shorthand. The typewriters were very heavy with manual carriages, and if we looked at the keys, we got our knuckles rapped by a ruler. At the end of each lesson we would have a bit of fun. The teacher would play the William Tell Overture on an old radiogram and we would type the prescribed exercises in time to the music. The further we got into the exercises, the faster the music would go. We started off in sequence with all the carriages being returned together along with the sound of the bells, but gradually the timing would go awry and in the finish we would all be in fits of laughter. It was a great way of building up your typing speed.

In our final year at school some of us girls had female German penfriends. One of our teachers had made an arrangement with a school in Hamburg, and six of us took up the invite to visit our penfriends for a month after leaving school and before starting work. This would be my first time abroad – boy, was I excited. Mum and Dad agreed to pay the fare, but I had to save up for my spending money. We went by train all the way from

London – the train went onto the ferry. We were met by our penfriends and their parents on arrival in Hamburg. Christiane was the name of mine and she lived with her mother, Gerda. Her father left when she was young, and she was an only child. All the families lived in apartments scattered in various parts of the city. It was arranged that we would all meet up to go to the Reeperbahn, famous for its nightlife and really the only place we wanted to go. We just had to visit the Star Club where the Beatles had recently played. We did eventually get to see it before returning to the UK, but imagine our dismay when we were only allowed to go heavily escorted by the parents and for a very limited period of time in the early evening. We did go to a dance, but boy, was it formal. We sat around the room, waiting for a German boy to come and ask one of us to dance. It wasn't long before they started to come over, and before I knew it a rather pimply boy appeared with his hand outstretched towards me. 'Please', he said, and he literally clicked his heels. I found it hard to refuse and therefore had to endure not one but a series of dances – mostly waltzes – before I could extricate myself. I certainly don't recall having any interesting or attractive dance partners that night. Another thing I wasn't too happy about was that my parents, along with my younger sister, had decided they would tour Germany by car and pay us a visit whilst passing through Hamburg. It had been raining heavily for days, and by the time they arrived, the campsite they intended to stay at was flooded. Gerda managed to get permission for them to sleep in the basement of the apartments. I'm not quite sure why now, but at the time I was so embarrassed about the whole thing. My kid sister Karen was four by then, and she befriended a little German boy who came regularly to play with her. He wore the traditional short leather trousers with the bib, and because of Karen's blonde hair she looked very German, especially once Mum clipped her plaited hair on top of her head. Selfishly, I was relieved when they continued their tour a few days later. I just wanted to be independent. It was there that I slept in a duvet for the first time, which I loved. I felt sorry for my friend Diane. Within a few days of arriving, the family she was with took her off camping in the Black Forest. What she didn't understand was that it was a nudist camp. She was so upset and nearly died of embarrassment when coming face to face with her penfriend's father starkers. Of all of us Diane was the most shy and modest. After three days of staying mostly inside the tent, the family finally got the message, cut short their holiday and headed back to Hamburg. We couldn't believe it when she told us on the way home, and we all agreed the family were very insensitive and stupid to have done such a thing.

Just before going off to Germany I went up to Liverpool Street in London and signed on with an employment agency. Alf Jones, my maths teacher, did his best to try and persuade me to go to college to continue my maths. University was out of the question as Mum and Dad couldn't afford that. He reckoned I would make a good maths teacher, but I just wasn't interested. All I wanted to do was to bash a typewriter in London. If he had said I could become an accountant and make loads of money, I might have taken more notice. He even came home and spoke to Mum and Dad about it. Dad just said I had my own mind and no way would he be able to persuade me otherwise. Although it was never said, I don't think they tried to change my mind because even going to college would have been difficult for them financially. Mind you, I did take after my dad by being strong-minded. I loved my dad to bits, but we often clashed.

When I returned from Germany there was a letter waiting for me from the employment agency. This was on a Friday and I had a job to go to the following Monday. That's how it happened back then as there were plenty of jobs available. It didn't enter my head that I may have difficulty getting work.

I was to be a junior secretary with a small travel insurance company, a subsidiary of Lloyds of London, based in the heart of the city. I was so excited. Mum and Dad agreed to pay for my first monthly train ticket to get me going. It was £5 which was quite a lot of money then. Chipping Ongar was right at the end of the Central Line. There was a single track to Epping where I would change for the train to Liverpool Street Station. It took just under an hour. Diane had also got a job nearby in the City, along with quite a few of my old classmates. So that's what I did for the next year. I was never a great timekeeper, so it wasn't unusual for one of my friends to jam their foot in the train door to stop it leaving whilst I tore down the platform. Most of us ended up catching the same train home, so we always made sure we ended up in the second-from-end carriage. As the train gradually emptied, we would gather together. If it was someone's birthday there would be cakes all round. Every now and again we would be entertained by a streaker or flasher. Being safe in numbers, these incidents were treated very light-heartedly, which probably didn't do much for the guy's ego. We also had to deal with the odd pervert who would rub himself up against us when we were all standing crammed together. I used to step back hard on their foot with the heel of my shoe and look up innocently, saying 'sorry'. I don't think any of us used to get upset about it; annoyed, yes. It was just part of the trials and tribulations of commuting, along with wading through all the rubbish dropped in the foot wells.

To begin with the commuting was great fun and I felt so grown up. I had started to smoke menthol cigarettes but rationed them to one for each journey. Health didn't come into the equation, but the cost certainly did. What little money I earnt had to go a long way. By the time I had paid for my monthly ticket and my weekly keep, there was little left for all the clothes and fun things I wanted to do. Going to pop concerts was out of the question. It was about this time that I decided to change my name from Teresa to Terri, and that was what I was known as from then on. Even Mum and Dad and my sisters ended up calling me Terri.

We got paid on a Friday, so a group of us would meet up in Lyons Corner House café in Oxford Street for a quick snack, and then we would browse the shops and often bought dangling earrings made out of your chosen beads at one of the many kiosks along the pavement. I hardly ever bought any clothes but would make lots of mental notes on what the latest fashions were for Mum to cleverly copy. I would buy the material during one of my lunch hours in Petticoat Lane, which was just round the corner from where I worked. It was in the heart of the Jewish community, and the butcher shops all had chickens hanging up outside with newspaper on the pavements to catch the blood that had to be drained from them.

Back to Friday nights; after browsing the shops we would then end up at the Tiles Club, which was about halfway down Oxford Street. It was below street level in some converted cellars, and quite the latest place to be. Scattered around the edges of the main floor were various bars and stalls where you could buy cheap jewellery, records, food and non-alcoholic drinks. You could even get your hair done at one place. Because of all the shops and bars it didn't cost a huge amount to get in. A lot of the sixties bands played there – Pink Floyd, The Moody Blues, Geno Washington and the Ram Jam Band, Stevie Wonder, and my absolute favourites The Rolling Stones, to name but a few. Many of the bands were just starting to make a name for themselves. It meant you could enjoy dancing to their music without loads of screaming going on and not be crowded out. I never did understand why girls screamed so much – crazy! Sadly, due to the level of drugs it used to get raided far too often. I think there was a lower cellar where a lot of the drug taking took place. Only once did we get caught up in one of the raids, but we managed to quickly leg it and avoid being caught. Not that we were doing anything wrong; none of us in our group were into drugs, and even if we were interested, not one of us was earning enough to afford to buy any.

To catch the last train to Ongar we had to leave Oxford Street at around 10.00 p.m. Rather than do that, we would catch a much later train that got us to Epping. We would then hitch-hike the last seven miles. All very risky as we were on the edge of the forest. None of our parents knew we did this – they all thought the other had picked us up. Only once did we get in a pickle. These guys picked two of us up, and just after we took off, a police car started to chase us. Instead of pulling over, the one driving floored it. We were petrified. They obviously knew the area well as the driver managed to lose the police car by turning off the main road into the dark area of North Weald Airfield, where they stopped and hit the lights. We ended up at one of their houses where they were expecting to have sex with us. Fortunately, when they realised we were not going to play along, they did the gallant thing and drove us to the top of our road. That was a big lesson for both of us. We were still quite young and inexperienced with life. After that we were a lot more cautious, and shortly afterwards another girl joined us whose father was a bit of a late nighter and therefore didn't mind picking us up.

Part of our pay packet included a luncheon voucher for each working day. They were worth 2s 6d – around twenty-five pence – each. For this you could get a roll, a packet of crisps and a yoghurt. When the weather was good, often Melanie, the other junior in the office, and I would grab our lunch and head on down to the Tower of London and sit by the riverbank in the sunshine. On one particular occasion we were madly chatted up by some Italian naval officers. On our way back to work

I commented, 'If that's a sample of the navy, I think I'll join up.' This was about a year after I started work. The thought stuck in my mind, and as each day passed, the smoky, dirty train journey started to get to me. I started to look around. I saw tired-looking faces. I listened to older girls discussing their boyfriends and when they were going to get married and start families. I began to appraise my own situation and ask myself what I wanted to achieve. Did I really want to carry on working in London until I met my future husband, then settle down to married life, probably somewhere not far away from Mum and Dad? Surely not when there was a whole world out there to explore. But how could I do this with such little money? Join the navy and see the world? Well why not.

I picked up some leaflets at a recruitment office in Liverpool Street and started to read through them. The more I read, the more I liked the idea. I kept getting butterflies in my stomach at the very thought of doing something different and exciting. I hadn't played any sport since leaving school and I missed it. The navy encouraged sport. You could be posted all over the place, not just within England but to amazing places like Gibraltar, Malta and Singapore. I then started to look at what type of job I could do. There was one that involved a lot of maths and outdoor work, which sounded perfect. The uniform wasn't that bad; okay, so a miniskirt was out, but it was a tight-fitting one and looked quite sexy, and I did suit navy blue. So, one lunch break, in a state of excitable nervousness, I went back to the recruitment office and had a chat with a very nice young male officer that resulted in me leaving in a very decided frame of mind and clutching various forms that needed filling in, including one that required a parent's permission. It was August, and I was not eighteen until the following month.

I couldn't wait to tell the girls on the train that night. When I did, the looks on their faces made me giggle. They were in shock and couldn't believe I was thinking of doing such a thing. I was really surprised at their reaction. It was so negative. I honestly thought that one or two might have wanted to come with me. It made me realise for the first time that I was kind of different in not being fazed by wanting to do something so out of the ordinary. It was probably just as well that I got that reaction as it prepared me a little for Mum and Dad's. Looking back, I realise that it must have been such a shock for them. Mum got all emotional, but Dad – well, he just started to rant. 'You'll hate it ... all those rules and regulations ... you're too rebellious ... you'll hate it!' Of course, being bullheaded and stubborn, and because it was my dad saying it, the more negative he became, the more determined I was to join up. Eventually and reluctantly, Dad finally signed the form which I promptly dropped into the recruitment office the following morning on my way to work. The category I chose was Range Assessor, which later changed to Weapons Analyst. I would be working with the Fleet Air Arm, which to me at the time sounded very glamorous. It wasn't long before I received a letter with an appointment for my medical. I can still remember what I wore on that day. It was a green crimplene minidress and jacket with patent yellow slingback shoes. I scoured the whole of Cheapside looking for those shoes, and they cost me two weeks' pay. Being fit and healthy I wasn't concerned about my medical. I was marked down as five feet five and a half inches, with green eyes. Next, I had to take an IQ exam, and before I knew it, I received a letter with a train ticket confirming my chosen job and instructions to report for Part I training on 1 November at HMS Burghfield near Reading. The year was 1966.

It was a Tuesday, and as it was a working day, Mum and Dad couldn't see me off. So, clutching a small case full of the things that were on the list that we could take, I caught the

Tube from Ongar to Waterloo Station in good time to catch the train to Reading. Upon arrival I was to look out for a naval bus to take us new recruits to Burghfield. By the time I reached Waterloo Station, the full realisation of what I was about to commit to kicked in. Up till then it was a whirl of excitable activity and saying goodbye to family, friends and work colleagues. The constant butterflies in my stomach went into overdrive and I started to shake a little. Suddenly I heard my name being called. I turned around and saw my dear Aunty Sylvia and Uncle Tom, who were also my godparents – a role they always took very seriously. They lived in Worcester Park, so it wasn't far for them to come. I was overwhelmed that they had taken the trouble to see me off, and had very tearful eyes when they scooped me up for a big hug. It was brilliant timing, and just what I needed to restore my courage and thirst for adventure. I loved them to bits.

The rest of the journey was a blur, and in no time at all I found myself amongst a group of girls standing outside the railway station, like me all feeling nervous and excited at the same time. Upon arrival at HMS Burghfield we were hustled into one of the wooden buildings and given an extremely unattractive navy blue below-knee wrap-around that was held together with an elastic money belt, and shown to our allotted dormitory in one of the wooden blocks. With the high wire fencing around the perimeter of the base, it reminded me of the prison camps seen in old wartime movies. We never did know if the fencing was to keep us girls in or the local lads out! It didn't seem to bother me that I was transformed from being a 1960s mini-clad dolly bird to looking like a cleaner woman down on her luck. There was worse to come.

Chapter 3 – Wren Experience

That first month, starting at 0600, I learnt how to scrub out toilets, wash a mountain of greasy pans, spit and polish shoes till they looked like patent leather, and march and jump to it when orders were barked by a petty officer. By week two, roughly a third of the squadron of forty girls had rushed back home, and we had swapped our skivvy outfits known as 'blues' for our smart naval uniforms. Out of the thirty or so left, only around twenty passed out. We made light of our menial tasks and a common bond built up between us. So much so, that when some of us met up fifty years later we all fell into easy conversation and found ourselves once again using many long-forgotten naval slang words and expressions. Making the decision to leave our homes, which were scattered nationwide, and step into an unknown and alien regimented life was not something many girls would have chosen to do. When it was lights out at 2200 we lit some candles we'd managed to get hold of and chatted and giggled away the dark hours. Once we were in uniform the menial tasks were left behind, and more time was spent in the classroom learning about the traditions of the navy, which was so much more fun.

There was method in their madness. To begin with we were reduced to the lowest of the low, which eliminated the nonstayers. Once the investment of providing us with a uniform happened, we were built up to feeling proud that we now belonged to the senior service. The marching – or 'square bashing', as it was called – continued, but was done with a lot more enthusiasm as we were all proud to do it in our smart uniforms complete with our black-seamed stockings that had to be ramrod straight. To this day my feet and arms will ache to move if I hear a recording of the Royal Marine band play 'Life on the Ocean Wave'. Before leaving, we had our second medical. When the doctor went to record the colour of my eyes he noted that previously they were recorded as being green. 'But they are most definitely blue,' he said. I then had to explain that they tended to change colour depending on what I was wearing. From then on the description of my eyes was down as 'green/blue'.

Before going onto our Part II training we were given leave to go home for a weekend. Dad was now well proud of his daughter, especially as I was about to tread in his footsteps by doing my category training at HMS Excellent in Whale Island, Portsmouth, where he also did his as a gunner during the war years. I loved my Part II training as a lot of mathematical calculations were involved. A causeway leads to Whale Island, at the end of which is the guard house. It was a sort of tradition that before the end of the training the Wren trainees were escorted by the 'three-badge stokers' for a run ashore. These were guys who have been in the navy for at least twelve years but have remained ordinary seamen. They tended not to be interested in any advancement or take responsibility, but they certainly knew all there was to know about the navy and were often regarded by all ratings as very useful guys to have around. Six or seven of us were taken out, and I reckon we must have visited every pub in that part of Portsmouth – and that was a lot. Virtually every street corner had a Brickwoods pub. This was when I was introduced to scrumpy with anisette chasers. That was some powerful mixture; how we managed to get across that causeway and safely back to the Wrens quarters without being put on a charge, I shall never know. I developed, and still have, a huge respect for those guys who, in return, always had a great respect for us Wrens. We instinctively knew that we would be well looked after and protected whilst ashore. They were – and probably still are – the navy's salt of the earth. Bless them all.

I was delighted when I got my orders after completing my Part II training. On 23 January 1967 I was to report to HMS Fulmar in Lossiemouth, which is in the Highlands of Scotland. This was the furthest base from where I lived, and it was the one place I was hoping I would be drafted to. The train went from Kings Cross to Edinburgh, where I had to change for one to Elgin, from where a Tilly (naval minibus) would take me to the base. It was an overnight sleeper, and I felt quite posh having dinner in the restaurant and even splashed out on a miniature bottle of Mateus rosé. I was too excited to sleep much, and once it became light I strained my neck to catch my first sight of mountains and snow from the train window. As we got closer to Edinburgh, I began to see snow by the side of the railway track. Most of the houses were built of grey stone rather than the red brick I was used to seeing, which made them look somewhat bleak but also quite austere. I spotted Edinburgh Castle miles before we reached the city. What an amazing sight coming into Edinburgh was. There were so many large, impressive buildings, overshadowed by the magnificent castle on the hill above the city. With very little delay we were on the Elgin train, and once Edinburgh was left behind the landscape changed. There were long stretches of coastline travel with dramatic bridges to the right, and over to the left more snow-capped mountains could be seen. Once we left the coast and headed inland towards Elgin, for the first time, I was astonished to see vast areas of bleak moors which fascinated me. As I was so used to being surrounded by many houses, this landscape was such a contrast and so alien to me. I kept staring out of the window hoping to see some deer, but no such luck. Taking in this incredibly bleak scenery overlooked by so many mountains, it suddenly struck me that I really was on a new adventure, and I was already loving every minute of it.

HMS Fulmar, also known as RNAS Lossiemouth, was quite an impressive base, and the Wrens quarters had been recently built. Each room had six beds, and there was even a dressmaking room, which I was delighted to see. Shortly after arriving we had a visit from Princess Margaret. I can't remember the reason for the visit – perhaps it was to do with our new quarters. When she inspected us, I was really surprised to see the thickness of her make-up and couldn't understand why she needed to apply so much. It was amusing to hear about the officer's orders that day. Princess Margaret would be having lunch at their mess, and although she had a habit of having a cigarette between courses, no officer was allowed to light up until coffee and brandy were served. Royal visits were not unusual at Lossie as often the Queen and Duke would fly in to visit their son Prince Charles, who was at the nearby school of Gordonstoun. If you were lucky and in the right place at the right time, you would catch a glimpse of them coming or going.

I was to work with 764, a training Hawker Hunter jet fighter squadron for pilots who eventually joined one of the front-line, carrier-borne Buccaneer squadrons. Unfortunately, there was a surplus of range assessors on the squadron, so it was a scramble to grab the work when it came in. In the meantime, we played an awful lot of Uckers – a naval version of the game of Ludo. It was a great relief when I was chosen to be the new range assessor for 801 Squadron. This was one of the final training squadrons for the Buccaneer pilots before they joined an aircraft carrier. I loved the work. Part of the time, we had to man Garvie Island, a live bombing range off Cape Wrath, Durness, which is close to being as far north as you can go, with John O' Groats not far away. Because live bombs were used it was the only range manned by naval personnel as opposed to civilians. It took well over three hours to get there by Tilly, but it was such an amazing journey. We went via Inverness, where we drove along the north edge of Loch Ness before going over the bridges that carried us across the Moray Firth. The route then took us north-west, passing many beautiful lochs. The closer we got to Durness, the bleaker the landscape became. There were many abandoned stone cottages, and I finally got to see my first wild deer. I kept thinking how dreadful it would be to break down in such a desolate place. It was, and still is, such wild and rugged countryside with little habitation. We even met one old lady there who only spoke Gaelic.

Our work involved taking cross bearings from two observation points. The main one was from a brick building across the beach that used to be an early warning radar station. The other observation point was in a small wooden hut situated across the bay and reached by Wessex helicopter; that is, if it was not called out on a search and rescue operation. When that happened we were taken across the bay by inflatable dinghy and then had a two-hour walk over the hills to get there. One time, two of us were flown over but were then left stranded. As we were expecting to be flown back, we didn't take our shoes with us as we tended to just stay in our rubber immersion suits – known as a goon suit. It was an all-in-one, including the boots which were always too big. The walk back over the hills was a real challenge. Due to lack of proper foot grip we did a lot of slipping and sliding over the rocks. From then onwards I always made sure an extra jumper and shoes were included in my pack when on these exercises.

Each strike consisted of a sortie of six Buccaneers – four carrying 1,000 lb bombs, with two as escorts. They often buzzed us during the exercise, which wasn't exactly helpful. The pilot would head towards the target, a rock off the coast marked with a large cross, and then pull up, tossing the bomb at a forty-five degree angle before getting the hell out of the area. This process was specifically designed for dropping nuclear bombs. Not only did we have to work out how close to the centre of the cross they hit, but once back at the squadron translate the results of a Hussenot trace: a series of dots and dashes that tracked how the aircraft functioned during the strike. It was one of the early types of flight recorder. From this you were able to establish why a pilot missed his target: for example, by going too fast, taking too steep a dive, or just being trigger happy. All pretty basic in today's technology, but you have to remember this was before compact computers; a computer in those days took up a whole room. One particularly exciting day, a trawler full of radar scanners and large aerials came into the outer danger area. It was obviously a Russian spy ship. The exercise was abandoned, resulting in a vast waste of money, and two of us were put on lookout duty, carefully plotting the trawler's movements which were then relayed on a hotline back to Admiralty headquarters in London. We stayed in a lovely guest house in the small hamlet of Durness and were well fed. I can still remember eating the home-baked scones topped with their own preserves, sitting around an open peat-fed fire. It was a bit naughty but, as it wasn't licensed for alcohol, if we were lucky enough to have the helicopter with us, we used to fly to the nearest bar which was in a small hotel quite a distance further down. I did smile when the media recently made such a fuss when Prince William misused one of the choppers. Enough said about that!

They say you should never volunteer for anything whilst in the services. Why wasn't I told this before I put my hand up? Six Wrens were asked to volunteer for a special exercise, and curiosity got the better of me. We were given goon suits to put on, and orange bags were strapped to our backs. We were then herded into a Wessex helicopter, and with very little briefing we found ourselves hovering over the Moray Firth. One by one we were pushed out of the open door of the helicopter into the sea, with the instruction to pull the cord which inflated the dinghy, and then unhook ourselves, climb into it, reattach ourselves to an inside hook, and wait. This was in February. Not having any gloves on, my fingers rapidly became numb, so it took quite a few attempts to unfasten myself from the outside hook which was underwater on the bottom of the dinghy. Trying to get into the dinghy wearing the cumbersome goon suit with the oversized boots was also quite a challenge. As they were only designed for men, there was a fly opening in the front which I soon discovered leaked. I can't remember how long I waited. All I can recall is that there I was, bobbing around in a small dinghy out of sight of anyone else, getting colder by the minute, and just to make matters worse, it started to snow. Eventually, and with great relief, I heard the Wessex return. I was then instructed by loudhailer to detach myself from the dinghy and hook up to the line that was lowered to me. Before I knew it I was hauled up into the chopper and, along with the others, flown back to base. We were each handed a can of soup – the survival type, whereby pulling the metal ring instantly heated the contents. Wonderful, thought I, until I tasted it. Who the hell decided to produce kidney soup? It was disgusting. The whole exercise left us girls quite baffled, until we heard later that it was a test to see who fared better – a bunch of girls or some junior lads. We never did find out the answer, but I like to think we won the bet. At least none of us appeared to have panicked.

Whilst I was still with 801 squadron, the Torrey Canyon disaster happened. A fully loaded supertanker hit a reef between the Cornish coast and the Isles of Scilly, causing a massive oil leak. It was decided that in order to break it up it should be bombed. First, the RAF hunters were called in, followed by the Fleet Air Arm, and some of my boys on 801 squadron took part. This was in March 1967, and with the look on their faces you would think Christmas had come again.

Whilst up in Scotland a few of us decided to write a letter to Pretty Polly hosiery company. Soon after miniskirts had come in they invented tights, but they were only in neutral brown shades. As part of our uniform we had to wear black stockings. For parade they had to have the seam going up the back, but for normal working hours we were allowed to wear the seamless micromesh ones which were far less of a pain to put on. In our letter to Pretty Polly we asked if they would consider making black tights, explaining the reason why. We received a lovely letter back saying they were looking into it, and in no time at all they were readily available, which was such great news. It wasn't long afterwards that tights in many colours and patterns came onto the market, and it became very trendy to wear them with micro miniskirts and dresses.

A few months later I was transferred to the Intelligence Centre. As weapons' analysts (our category name had changed by then) we were cleared to handle top security information. This made us ideal candidates for being seconded into Intelligence, as personal vetting had already been done. I enjoyed being there, as one of my duties was to quiz the pilots on their recognition skills with Russian ships and aeroplanes. Especially exciting was the time when we did an invasion exercise which created a hive of activity in what was normally a very quiet environment. I was kept on my toes, providing all sorts of information stored in our safes to a group of officers seated round a large table. It was quite nerve-racking to have so much gold braid in one room. Another duty of mine was to look after any visiting pilots who used the centre as their base. An American chap who had brought over one of the Lightning F6 jet fighters joined us on a couple of nights out, and popped in for his final cup of coffee before leaving. Two hours later he came back in looking a little shaken but with a gleam in his eye. 'Great – now I get my tie,' he announced. Shortly after taking off he found the jet had a fault and tried to head back to Lossiemouth, but unfortunately couldn't make it in time and had to bail out before the plane crashed in a field close to the caravan park where a lot of the service men's families lived. My God! It could so easily have been such an awful disaster.

While I was working at the Intelligence Centre, I did something that was not clever of me at all and got me into some serious trouble. I joined the ski club, and each weekend during the winter season a group of us would head up to Aviemore straight after secure (finishing work, for you non-naval lot) on the Friday. Every now and again we would have what was known as a long weekend when Monday was included as a day off too. My final duty each day was to properly secure the Intelligence Centre and hand in the keys to the gunnery office which was at the main gate. As the Wren's quarters were en route, I stopped off to change and grab my weekend bag, throwing the Intelligence Centre keys into my civilian handbag. One of the pilots was waiting to pick me up in his car, and off we went, being smartly saluted as we left through the main gate. The routine was that we all gathered at The Grant Arms Hotel in Grantown. The kitty for drinks was sorted out beforehand, and while everyone had a drink or two, one car would carry on to the caravans – with the food given to us from the mess deck – and start a 'pusser's' stew, where tins of whatever we had been given went into a big pot. This usually consisted of beef, tomatoes, baked beans, potatoes and various veggies. It was our turn to do this, so, chucking my handbag on a corner shelf in the caravan on arrival, I put my mind to preparing the stew. After supper we all went off to a couple of local hotels for some Scottish dancing, and we were up early the following morning, as usual keen to hit the slopes. Goodness, what stamina we had then!

It was halfway through the morning, whilst skiing down the Shieling pass, that I took a tumble and decided to take a break at the halfway house. There at the entrance was a board and easel with a message: 'Will Wren Pegg report in immediately'. As soon as I saw the message I realised what it meant. 'Oh my God, the keys!' I said to a friend who was skiing with me (we would never go it alone). I ran to the phone box, grabbed the phone with shaking hands and dialled the base. As soon as I said my name, I was put through to the duty officer. I was to get back to the caravans right away and a Tilly would collect me. The base was two hours away from the caravans, and we were another thirty minutes from them. I had to find the driver of the gypsy – a four-wheel drive vehicle that we used to get up to the slopes in. Fortunately, just as I was wondering how the hell I could find him, he walked in. What luck, as he could have been anywhere on the slopes, and of course mobile phones were non-existent then.

The chap who I was skiing with offered to come with me. He was a naval dentist and was happy to take a break. Once I had dropped back the keys, he would pick up his car so that we could return for the rest of the long weekend. On our way back to base in the Tilly, every now and again a policeman stopped us to ask if we had Wren Pegg on board. I was beginning to realise I was in serious trouble. By the time we arrived at the main gate I was trembling like a leaf. We were pounced on, and I was told to change into my No. 1 uniform and report to the duty officer. The chap who came with me, whose name I cannot remember now, said he would get in touch once he found out a little more back in the wardroom. He called me just as I was about to head off to the duty officer. 'Good lord,' he said. 'What a rumpus. I'm afraid there's no chance of you returning to Aviemore. Everyone is up in arms about the whole thing. Sorry, Terri, but there's nothing I can do. Good luck.' That really got my knees shaking. Oh my gawd, I thought, I really have done it this time. When I arrived at the duty office I was confronted not only by the current duty officer but also the previous day's duty officer, my divisional officer and my direct boss who was a lieutenant commander. They had all been summoned back from their long weekend leaves. That's when I really started to panic, and I'm sure my face must have been white as a sheet.

The previous day's duty officer was one of the ski members, and as soon as he realised my keys were missing, he guessed right away what had happened. He tried to reach me, or any of the group, at the various hotels but kept missing us, and there was no telephone at the caravans. It left him with no option but to raise the alarm. Guards were put on duty at the Intelligence Centre, and there was a full security alert. They even sent up a helicopter the following morning to search the slopes, trying to spot any of us clad in our naval anoraks. I was vaguely aware of a helicopter buzzing around that morning but didn't pay it much attention. After cross-examining me, and thanks to the support of my boss (he was a real sweetie) and my divisional officer, it was decided that I would be going on First Officer's Defaulters for negligence. I hadn't broken any Captain's Standard Orders, but, apparently, I was very nearly going to be used as an example and be court-martialled for breaking the Official Secrets Act. How frightening and serious was that. I could have gone to prison! And all because I had forgotten to give in a bunch of keys. It happened all the time with stores, but of course their keys were not important, and therefore there was no consequence if they were not handed in. I was given the maximum of thirty days' stoppage of leave. This meant that as soon as I finished work for the day, I had to remain in uniform and report to the duty officer on the hour, every hour, until 2200 when I had to go to bed. During the weekend it was every two hours from 0800 until 2200, once again still in uniform. As I was deemed irresponsible to continue working at the Intelligence Centre, I was sent back to 764 Squadron.

I was told that the punishment was to commence straight after the long weekend, meaning Tuesday at 0800 hours. So, I had two days of freedom before my ordeal began. I didn't do much on the Sunday. I was still trying to get over the shock of what had happened and the realisation that being restricted to the Wren's quarters in my spare time, especially during the weekends, was going to send me insane. I am not a person who can just sit and do nothing. I have to keep busy. But then, I had an idea. For a while now I had been wanting to buy a cloak, which was becoming fashionable. I had also recently watched the film Bonnie and Clyde and loved the idea of wearing a Bonnie-type outfit for a change from the miniskirts. Why not make full use of the dressmaking room and create my own? First thing Monday I caught the bus into Elgin and headed straight to the fabric shop. I managed to get a pattern for a cloak and a blouse that I was able to alter into the style I had in mind. I already had a pattern for the skirt; I just needed to extend the length to below the knee. I found some mustard yellow material for the cloak, and a tweedy mauve and pink fabric for the skirt, with some paler pink cotton for the blouse. I then headed over to the haberdashery department where I completed my purchases with all the trimmings, cottons and so on. On the bus, on my way back to the base, I felt really chuffed with my successful shop and was beginning to get excited at the prospect of making the garments. I was definitely turning a disaster into a more positive action, and thanks to this my punishment time did not seem so daunting; in fact, it seemed to pass quite quickly. I loved wearing my new outfits and received some great compliments. I certainly had my mum's and nan's genes when it came to dressmaking. As a child I never really played with dolls; I was far more interested in how they were put together and made use of them to practise by making clothes for them out of scraps of spare material. Mum and Dad knew back then that I was definitely more of a tomboy who would happily bang nails into a piece of wood rather than walk around with a doll in a pram.

Chapter 4 – Life-Changing Loves

Apart from my harrowing experience with the keys, I thoroughly enjoyed my time up in Scotland. I was there for nearly two years. Shortly after arriving, I started to date David, a young leading hand who came from Yorkshire. I loved his accent and we instantly got on well. He was a really good-looking chap and was in the football team. He was mad about the game and was a great player. I think Sheffield Wednesday were interested in him, but he decided to join the navy instead. After only a few months we got engaged, and that was when I lost my virginity. I was nineteen and David was twenty, and we both felt we understood what love was all about. David had a car but was still a learner. This was not a problem as I had my full driving licence. For my sixteenth birthday my mum and dad bought me six driving lessons, and on a few occasions when my dad was working up in London on a site I would meet him at Liverpool Street Station to drive us home in the rush hour. He reckoned that if I could learn to drive under those circumstances, then I would be okay to drive anyway in the world. As it turned out, he was so right.

Shortly after David and I announced our engagement to our respective parents we drove to Gomersal, which is near Leeds, to meet his family. It was quite a weird weekend. On Saturday afternoon we went to watch Leeds football team play at home, and Dave's dad insisted that I drove. It could have been quite daunting to drive in such a busy, unknown city, but thanks to my dad's driving philosophy I didn't panic, and I think I did okay; at least, his dad didn't make any comment and I was convinced he was testing me. Then, on Sunday, Dave's mum asked me to make the Yorkshire pudding. Me, a southerner, asked to make their own regional dish. How could she? She stood over me, telling me what to do. Once again I distinctly felt I was being tested. I smoked back then, but David didn't. Being totally insensitive to the fact I was in a non-smoking house, I lit up during the evening. Big mistake. It was the only time David got really cross with me; not for actually smoking, which obviously did not go down at all well with his folks, but for not emptying the ashtray afterwards.

For me the weekend was a total disaster; so much so, that about a week after returning to base, I broke off the engagement. I just knew it wasn't going to work out, and by then I was working on 801 Squadron which was full of young, good-looking, fun guys. I had my own small office off the hangar, and, as the only female, I was loving being the centre of attention and was starting to take interest in one or two of them. How could I do that when I was supposed to be in love with someone else? I know I upset David at the time, but it was the right thing to do. I often wonder how he made out and hope he ended up happily married with a loving family. I did meet him briefly about three years later in The Jolly Roger pub down in Gosport. I had just returned from a sailing trip, and the rest of the crew and I were having a drink or two in our favourite pub. I didn't notice David was there until he came over just before leaving. He took me by surprise and left quickly. I would have liked to have met up with him for old times' sake, but perhaps that wouldn't have been such a good idea, especially as he had a girl in tow.

After breaking off the engagement I joined the ranks of being classed as 'pig's meat'. Not a very pleasant description, is it? It was the name given by the lower ranks to Wrens who dated officers. That was when Sandy and I became good friends. She was dating one of the pilots and we often went out as a foursome. The first one I dated was Alan, who at nineteen – the same age as me – was the youngest Buccaneer pilot. In retrospect that was such a young age for someone to be flying a powerful jet capable of low-level speeds of between five and six hundred knots and landing on an aircraft carrier. Another chap I dated for a while was Roger. He was such great fun in a roguish sort of way. All the pilots were a bit mad and definitely brainwashed. Favourite haunts of theirs for weekend lunchtime drinking were either the Thunderton in Elgin or the Gordon Arms in Fochabers. Walking into a room full of them, you would witness a sea of arms waving about illustrating their flying techniques. They talked of little else. Socially, it was probably the best time of my life. They all had fast cars and, as a group, we wouldn't think twice about driving halfway across Scotland for a decent roast beef Sunday lunch. Wrens were not allowed in their own wardroom, so a group of us would go over to RAF Kinloss for their weekly curry night. There was always a party somewhere or other at weekends where we drank and danced a lot. We were allowed to request a SOP (sleeping out pass) or a late pass (midnight instead of 2200) but if we had either forgotten or had a change of heart, we would do a bunk instead. I was in a ground floor dorm at the back of the Wrens quarters. We always left one of the large windows open, and at weekends there would be a constant stream of girls coming and going. We would sign in before 2200 and then skip out the window. Unfortunately, on one occasion, a junior lad on patrol witnessed one of the girls climbing out and thought it was his duty to report it. What an idiot. A bed check was done and more than thirty girls were missing. All hell broke loose. Fortunately, I was on a SOP that night.

A lot of us Wrens smoked. The men were allowed three hundred duty-free cigarettes each month which made them very cheap to buy. Unfairly, Wrens were not granted the same dispensation, and in fact if we were caught with any, we ran the risk of being court-martialled on a charge of smuggling, which was a bit extreme. They were called 'blue liners' due to the blue line printed down the length of each cigarette. This didn't stop us Wrens getting hold of them. We used to put them into an Embassy packet and had to smoke them right down to the tip to ensure all of the blue line was burnt on the butts. How revolting, and so unhealthy.

One of the reasons I joined up was because of the sporting opportunities. I started to play badminton and squash and took up shooting. To begin with it was indoor .22 rifles, but then I progressed to using an SLR which was short for 'self-loading rifle' and was the standard troop gun at the time. I was a keen shot and ended up being the only female in the rifle team. We would practise up on the ranges in all weather, sometimes getting into the sacks used for laying on when there was snow on the ground. One time when we arrived there were some juniors on the range before us. They were using a variety of weapons including Bren guns. All of a sudden one of the lads turned around holding his gun, shouting to the chief that it was stuck. It was stuck in the firing position. You never saw so many of us hit the deck so quickly. Stupid boy! Another time the range officer suddenly shouted to us to change target to one o'clock. Turning around, I saw a beautiful stag on the horizon. Much to my relief, it scarpered before anyone had a chance to shoot it.

I did do one Browndown Range meet which was held in Gosport, back in Hampshire. Four of us drove down in one car with all the rifles and ammo in the boot. There would have been some explaining to do if we had been stopped by the police, especially as we were travelling at night out of uniform. I can't see that sort of thing happening today! On a couple of occasions I was flown down in one of the de Havilland Devon transport planes for sport – once for a game of badminton, and then again for a softball match. I remember walking into HMS Dryad in Portsmouth wearing my uniform but also long black boots. The duty officer hauled me in for doing so and wouldn't believe me when I said that as a special dispensation for being stationed in Scotland, we were allowed to wear boots during the winter months. Even after phoning the station to check, she was reluctant to let me off – probably due to my cockiness!

Shortly after being sent back to 764 Squadron in disgrace following the keys incident, I was transferred down to HMS Daedalus in Lee-on-Solent, which was the Fleet Air Arm's headquarters. Once again I found myself in the Intelligence section and, surprise, surprise, having the same responsibility of handing in the department's keys at the end of the day to the guard house. The only difference this time was that I was on a rota with four other girls. At first I was heartbroken at leaving not only Scotland but also Roger. It wasn't a mad, passionate love affair, but we did have a lot of fun together. I also left just before the ski season began, which was a big disappointment. I was so looking forward to improving my skills up on the slopes. I soon cheered up once I got stuck into the work as I found it fascinating. The department gathered geographical information worldwide and stored the information on punch cards which also included microfilms. This was the forerunner of collecting data on a computer. We used a machine that had a standard typewriter keyboard, where we typed in the information, given to us in paper form, onto a set of cards. The outcome was a row of punched holes which could be deciphered into the information we had punched in. The same set of cards was then put into a correction machine, repeating what we had done. This was to check for mistakes. If there were any, the machine would spit out the card. Once the mistakes were corrected, the cards were run through a machine that added the microfilms which had to be in the correct order. Finally, there was a copy machine in case more than one set was needed, which was often the case.

Once it was discovered my typing speed was fast, I was soon given the job of operating these machines. I then started to investigate how they worked by studying the command panels. Each one had a metal panel with double-ended wires going into various holes. I soon worked out by experimenting that I could get one machine talking to another, which speeded up the whole process. Due to confidentiality, the room had to be locked at all times and access was restricted. I was in my element, locked in this room playing with these fascinating machines, and surprisingly never got bored, as I found the information I was typing in very interesting. I was learning about all sorts of places worldwide.

The department was run by a retired commander – a really lovely old boy. Mid-morning one hot summer's day, he threw down his pen and declared it was far too hot to work. He then phoned the outward-bound section and requested a yacht with a skipper to take him and his girls sailing that afternoon. In those days someone of his position got away with such things. He arranged a Tilly to take us down to the Hornet Services Sailing Club in Haslar Creek where one of the naval yachts Swordfish was ready for us to board, and that was when I first met Roy Williams who was assigned to be our skipper. In no time at all, with Roy's guidance we let go of the ropes and raised the sails. This was my first experience of sailing, and it was love at first sight. I have always enjoyed anything to do with water and was a good swimmer. In his youth Dad was brought up in

Thorpe Bay, just along the coast from Southend on Sea, and swam for Essex. He used to put my younger sister Janet and me on his back when we were quite young, and swim out and then encourage us to doggy paddle back, with Mum watching anxiously from the beach. Sitting in Swordfish's cockpit, the feeling of the warm, gentle breeze on my face, and listening to the whooshing sound of the yacht slicing through the waves, was heavenly. I was totally mesmerised watching the water passing by, and when we headed up into the wind with the sails pulled in, causing the boat to heel over, it was so exhilarating. My eyes welled up with the sheer emotion of it, and no one could get any conversation out of me. I just didn't want it to end; but sadly, far too quickly the sails were down, and we were motoring back up the creek to Hornet.

Whilst we were waiting for the Tilly to return I had a chat with Roy. There was something about the guy that I liked. He wasn't good-looking – he was on the short side and quite a lot older – but his weathered face and twinkling blue eyes were very appealing. I was impressed with his laid-back attitude when confronted with a bunch of girls who knew nothing about sailing, along with our dear boss who was no help at all. His name was familiar, but it took me a while before I remembered why. Just before leaving Scotland, one of the members of the ski club suggested that, as I couldn't continue to ski down south, I might like to think about sailing, and should look up Leslie and Roy Williams. They were not brothers; they just happened to have the same surname. I mentioned this to Roy and passed on Smudge Smith's regards, and said how much I would love to learn to sail. 'Not a problem,' he said. 'Come down on Saturday if you like – see you here about ten.'

The next three days couldn't pass quickly enough. I decided to wear a swimsuit with shorts and a T-shirt over the top, which I hoped was the right gear and would fit in with everyone else.

It was raining but that didn't worry me; I would probably get wet anyway. What I hadn't taken into account was that, along with the rain, there was no wind – quite an essential ingredient if you want to sail. Unbeknownst to me, because of the weather conditions, the guys at the sailing club were taking bets as to whether I would turn up or not. Feeling very nervous, I took a deep breath and pushed open the door to the clubhouse. I received a warm welcome although I was somewhat puzzled by those who had really big smiles. They then kindly explained to me that, with virtually no wind, there would not be any sailing lessons that day, but that I could become familiar with the boat. It was a 14 ft fibreglass Bosun dinghy of which there were a few. They were specifically built for naval use. Between us we took three of them out, and my first sailing lesson was how to paddle one as fast as possible in order to get to The Jolly Roger in Hardway in time for a lunchtime drink or two. That was the start of what was to become a major change in my life. The year was 1968.

From then on, every weekend you would find me down at Hornet. It used to be a naval base for coastal forces, and after it was disbanded in the 1950s it was used by the navy, initially to house a number of random yachts including those that were taken from the Germans at the end of the war. They were known as windfalls and included the two allocated to the navy to be used for sail training, Merlin and Marabu. As a chief petty officer, Roy was the sail training officer. Gradually, my sailing skills improved enough for me to join in with racing the Bosuns, and I even did the frostbite season. I can well remember banging ice out of the ropes so we could use them. Even when the bitter wind would rip through the many layers of clothes, and fingers would become numb with the cold, it never put me off. Helming was not really my thing. I was far more comfortable crewing and became very adept at handling the sails. In addition to that, I loved helping out on the yachts – scrubbing the decks, cleaning the insides, polishing brass, and even doing some of the varnishing. In return I got to crew on occasions when a girl was allowed on board. Believe it or not, back then Wrens were not allowed to serve on ships. We were kept firmly ashore until the 1990s when the navy finally gave in to female equality.

Navy week in Portsmouth Dockyard was coming up, and I was invited to join the team that would be based on Spirit of Cutty Sark. It was an unofficial one, and therefore I didn't need to be in uniform. The yacht was a Gallant 53 that Leslie Williams raced in the Single-Handed Trans-Atlantic Race earlier on that year. Normally, this design of boat was rigged as a ketch, but Leslie had it changed to a sloop with the main mast considerably higher. Although the main was therefore harder to handle, it was a good deal faster under most wind conditions. He did amazingly well, coming in fourth overall, and was the first production boat in. I hadn't yet met Roy's partner in crime, Leslie, who, although still serving in the navy as a lieutenant, was kept busy giving various talks around the yacht clubs after the race. Spirit of Cutty Sark was to be exhibited along with Francis Chichester's Gypsy Moth IV. He was the first to sail solo around the world, for which he received a knighthood. I used some of my leave and booked into the Serviceman's club nearby, avoiding having to travel back and forth from Lee-on-Solent.

Portsmouth, as I'm sure many of you will know, is the hub of the navy. Although I had promised myself to visit the dockyard since being drafted south, up till now I had not done so. I had of course seen photos of the place, but being there in person was amazing. I stood inside the entrance looking around me, in particular at the incredibly well-preserved HMS Victory which was Nelson's flagship. It was hard to believe that she had been built over two hundred years ago, and survived not only the battle of Trafalgar during the Napoleonic Wars but also lead the fleet into the War of American Independence and the French Revolution. So much history. I spotted both Spirit of Cutty Sark and Gypsy Moth IV not far away, tied up next to each other along the main dock. Before going over I decided to spend a little time wandering around the dockyard, taking in the many centuries of naval history. It certainly made me feel proud that I was part of her Majesty's senior service. The place was buzzing with so many people. I wanted to go on board Victory but the queue was far too long. Hey ho – another day. Feeling slightly nervous, I eventually headed towards Cutty Sark.

What a week it turned out to be. Spirit of Cutty Sark was sponsored by Cutty Sark whisky, and there appeared to be an endless supply of the stuff on board. In a rather alcoholic haze, I allowed Leslie to seduce me. Who could resist such beautiful brown, doleful eyes. After that week we spent a lot of time together. He was eighteen years older than me and divorced, and had custody of his two children. He had such a way with women – he was a magnet; they just swooned all over him. I found this all rather amusing and felt quite flattered that I was the current favourite, especially as some of them were well-groomed, sophisticated ladies, one or two of them being BOAC hostesses. And there was I, who hardly ever wore make-up, kept my hair short because I couldn't be bothered with it, and ashamedly bit my nails. I really was quite a tomboy. He certainly didn't remain faithful, but that didn't bother me as our relationship was quite a free and easy one. I think I was more in love with the lifestyle that was developing.

Weekends were often spent sailing Spirit of Cutty Sark. By 1700 on the Friday we would slip our moorings and sail across to Cherbourg. There would usually be about six of us on board, with me being the only female. It would take around twelve hours, and if we were lucky, we would have caught some mackerel on a trailing line. I can still taste those breakfasts of grilled fish with freshly baked baguettes from the nearby patisserie in the harbour. Once we were cleared by customs and immigration and got our green card stamped, we would pick up our duty-free wine and, if the tides were right, sail over to Alderney in the Channel Islands. We would always end up on Saturday night at the Railway Tavern which was our favourite eating/drinking hole there. Staggering along the railway track in the dark to find our way back to the harbour was always a challenge. The Channel Islands are notorious for their fall of tides, which can be as much as thirty to forty feet. We would anchor in the harbour and use our dinghy to get to the harbour wall, where we would then have to climb up a rusty metal ladder. Not easy to do in sailing boots and foul weather gear, which invariably is the case. Returning in the dark and under the influence when the tide is low becomes even more of a challenge, but somehow no one ended up in the thick mud below. We did have one particularly harrowing experience on our return trip back to Portsmouth. We would normally leave Alderney late afternoon on the Sunday, and this was no exception. However, it was thick fog all the way – we couldn't even see the bow from the cockpit. Even with at least four experienced navigators on board it was scary for all of us. We could hear ships' horns constantly sounding all around, and just prayed that our radar reflector was working well and that all ships were on red alert. None of us slept on the way back, and all eyes were strained from keeping an all-round lookout. It was with great relief that we entered the harbour mouth when the shore lights helped to lift the fog a little.

I'm not sure how it really happened, but when Leslie was away for a few weeks, giving further talks around the various yacht clubs and naval bases, Roy and I started spending more and more time together. Although he was still married, he had already split with his wife, and he had a son who I think was about ten. The inevitable happened, and we became very much an item. The twenty years' difference in age never seemed to be an issue to us, and I was beginning to fall in love with him. I think I had an inkling this would eventually happen from the first time we met on Swordfish. Apart from me having such overwhelming emotions in discovering sailing, there was definitely a spark between us. He originally came from Shropshire, and was very down to earth and so laid-back. Although there was a lot of teasing between us all, I don't think Leslie was too put out when he discovered our relationship upon his return, for there were always plenty of other girls to choose from. The sixties were like that.

For Roy and me it was the start of a long-term relationship. I had fallen in love big time and just wanted to be with Roy constantly. All previous relationships became insignificant – this was the real thing. Each weekend couldn't come around quickly enough as I hated having to go back to the Wren's quarters at night during the week.

The time had come to introduce Roy to my parents, and I must admit it was a bit daunting. Knowing our age difference was going to be a shock to them, in my telephone conversation with Mum beforehand I mentioned this fact. I have to say I take my hat off to them. Although underneath they must have been quite dismayed – for goodness sake, Roy was only two years younger than my mum – they were so good about it. Roy is a very likeable person, and it wasn't long before conversation easily flowed. Mind you, there was no sleeping together. That would have been just too much for my folks to cope with. Both my sisters were a bit bemused. Janet, who was two years younger than me, was going steady with Richard, who she had known since primary school. My kid sister Karen – thirteen years younger – didn't quite know what to say. In her eyes he was an old man.

Chapter 5 – Adventure Beckons

Within a few weeks of going out with Roy I was summoned to First Officer Wren's office with the order to report in my No. 1 uniform. What the hell? As far as I knew, I hadn't broken any regulations and I'd done nothing wrong at work. Okay, so I had made full use of my allocated sleeping out and late passes, but so what? The last kit inspection was okay; we soon wised up to them by buying a leaving Wren's decent kit and not touching it. That way, everything would be in perfect condition. The spare pair of flat shoes – known as 'square bashers' – would be kept in an old pair of stockings to help retain their required patent leather condition. We would also keep a spare pair of black court shoes with unscratched heels. By then we were allowed to wear black tights, but we still had to use the black-seamed sheer stockings for parade, and three pairs were required for kit muster. Of course everything had to have your name on it, including three vests – part of the kit that no one would be seen wearing, ever.

In trepidation I knocked on the door at the requested time and walked smartly in, giving my best salute. I was astounded to see not only the First Officer, but my divisional officer and the commander of the base. Oh gawd, what now? With a grave sense of déjà vu, I stood to attention until told to 'stand at ease'.

I was then informed that it had come to their attention that I was dating a married man, and as I had signed the Official Secrets Act, they were deeply concerned. This was the last thing I expected, and, without thinking, I blurted out 'Why?' which embarrassingly came out as just a squeak.

I quickly pulled myself together and said, 'Sorry, Ma'am. Might I ask why you are concerned?'

'Because, you stupid girl, you have left yourself wide open to blackmail.'

I was incensed at being told I was stupid, but it gave me the strength to reassure them that this would definitely not happen. I informed them that my relationship with Chief Petty Officer Roy Williams was common knowledge, including for his wife. They were separated; she was dating a RAF officer and had recently asked for a divorce. I was then asked to wait outside. When I was called back in I was informed that no further action would be taken, but that this information would be recorded on my records. It was with great relief I was then dismissed. I left that office with a mixture of emotions. I was still furious at the way they spoke to me, but I was also alarmed at the way they chose to handle the situation. It was done in such a formal way and felt rather like some sort of inquest.

Shortly after this Roy and Leslie put their heads together to decide what to do with Spirit of Cutty Sark. It had to make money, as no way could Leslie afford to keep it just for personal use. The deal with Cutty Sark whisky was that after the race, Leslie and the boat were to be at their disposal for PR and marketing purposes until the end of the summer of 1969. After that, the boat belonged to Leslie. He still had another two years to serve in the navy, and as he had had so much time off already, the pressure was on for him to get back to doing his job. Roy was due to complete his twenty-two-year service at the end of September. So, it was agreed that Roy would sail it to the West

Indies for chartering in time for the 1969/1970 season and then bring it back to Europe for the following summer season. Spirit of Cutty Sark was built at Southern Ocean Shipyard in Poole. Two further Gallant 53s were built and delivered to Friendship Bay Hotel in Bequia, part of St Vincent and the Grenadines in the Windward Islands of the West Indies. Through that connection, Roy managed to get the job of looking after these yachts, along with various dinghies and sailboards belonging to the hotel, for the forthcoming season. The idea was to familiarise himself with the area and find out how best to market Spirit of Cutty Sark for chartering during the following season, assuming it was at all feasible and worthwhile financially.

The news came as a big blow to me. I was devastated that I would not see Roy for six months and was full of doom and gloom as to what kind of future we would have together. Would our relationship survive the separation? Roy felt quite positive about us and what lay ahead, but I was not convinced. For me, yes, but Roy had come with quite a reputation for the ladies. So far he had remained faithful; at least, I think so, but I was not convinced this would remain the case, if and when temptation came his way. All this I kept to myself as I didn't want to create a cloud over our relationship before he departed. We said our goodbyes in Lee-on-Solent as I couldn't bear going to the airport. I then spent quite a few tearful days before giving myself a good talking-to. In those days we wrote letters to communicate. Skyping didn't exist, and the telephone which had only recently been installed on the island of Bequia was slow, poor quality, and expensive.

I kept myself busy, and for a while I was a model Wren, working hard and rarely requesting a SOP or late pass. During this time I did my Leading Wrens two-week course back at HMS Excellent at Whale Island. I continued going down to Hornet, helping out where I could, and still did the frostbite season racing Bosuns as a crew member. The yachts, including Spirit of Cutty Sark, were laid up for the winter months. I was overjoyed to discover Roy was a great letter writer. They were full of interesting information with lots of funny anecdotes, and surprisingly and touchingly romantic which I wasn't expecting. However, they were not very frequent: one every two to three weeks. I was constantly checking my mailbox, and my heart would leap when I spotted a blue and white airmail envelope. I would deliberately wait until I was sitting down comfortably in a quiet spot with a cup of coffee and a cigarette so that I could enjoy and savour reading every word. I made it policy not to write to Roy until I received a reply to my previous letter. I didn't want to bombard him with too many and put him under pressure to write more often. In any case, my news was nothing like as interesting as his. I was missing him so much.

My lifestyle had become so mundane compared to his. Before Roy left, he had two cars – a souped-up Mini Cooper with lower suspension and wide wheels, and a minivan. His ex-wife, Sandra, was given the Mini Cooper as part of the divorce settlement, and I got the rusty old minivan, which suited me well. It was great to have my own car for the first time, and I didn't care what it was as long as it had four wheels and worked; well, just about. One particular evening I lost track of time down at the clubhouse at Hornet and consequently drove far too fast along the coastal road back to base at Lee-on-Solent. I was determined not to be late. The roads were a bit icy and I lost it on a bend, resulting in spinning the car and ending up facing the wrong way with two of the wheels in a shallow ditch. Damn and double damn when I noticed a police car parked off-road just before the bend. They slowly walked towards me. I was sure I was going to get a ticket for dangerous driving. Instead they checked to make sure I was all right and then helped me bump the van out of the ditch. Making the correct assumption that I was rushing back to base before the 2200 deadline, they offered to escort me back and explain that, due to having been shaken up after hitting some ice, they had to detain me for a while; hence the reason why I was late. I couldn't believe my luck and was so grateful to them. I didn't want to yet again find myself on defaulters and have one or two stoppage of leave days. My impulse was to give both of them a big hug, but with the guard house watching I had to just shake their hands. With grins and a wink they went on their way.

The official sailing season out in the West Indies was from 15 December to 15 April. During that time the trade winds are settled, with little fear of hurricanes and tropical storms, making it absolutely perfect sailing weather. Roy planned to return by the end of April. I therefore was devastated when he informed me in a letter, which I thought would be his final one, that he had accepted a delivery job to take a yacht up to Puerto Rico. This would delay his return by about four to six weeks. Up till then I was counting the days, not months. I spent quite a few days down in the dumps before getting over the disappointment. He finally returned in the middle of June. By then the yachts were back in action and I had done a couple of weekend sails on Spirit of Cutty Sark. It was so wonderful having Roy back. It felt as though my life had been on hold but was now back to normal. He still loved me and had missed me a lot. I was so relieved and so very happy. He hadn't changed at all, except his dark brown hair now had blonde streaks in it as if he had dipped his comb in peroxide. And of course he was a few shades browner than the rest of us.

There was a lot of celebration down at The Jolly Roger pub in Hardway which had become virtually our second home. The landlord, Bill Elgie, his wife, Thelma, and son, Roger, had become great friends. It was after a particularly heavy drinking session that once again I found myself in trouble. Roy and I had decided to stop on the way back to base. We did no more than cuddle up watching the ocean, parked up at Stokes Bay, but then promptly fell asleep. Drinking and driving was the norm in those days. The next thing we knew, it was 12.30 a.m. Boy, was I going to get it. I was of course reported and the following day, once again in my No. 1 uniform, I stood in front of First Officer Wrens with my divisional officer present. When asked why I was late, I told the truth. I was grateful to my divisional officer who spoke up for me by stating that I was very apologetic to everyone at the guard house when I did arrive back. I think she did this as I knew she was quite keen to get in with the sailing crowd. She always made envious remarks every time she signed off my request for a weekend pass to go sailing. I only got one day's stoppage of leave that time, and as a thank you, I mischievously gave her Leslie's phone number. Well, she was pretty, so I knew he wouldn't have objected.

Sadly, it was shortly after that confrontation that I was once again summoned by the First Officer with the same monotonous rigmarole. Blimey – what now? This was getting really ridiculous, as once again I didn't have a clue what it was all about. This time I was addressed by just my surname: Pegg. That set off an alarm bell in my head, and what happened next left me completely in shock. I was informed that I would not be suitable to represent the Wrens abroad. When asked if I wanted to make a comment, I just shook my head and said, 'No, Ma'am.' I couldn't get out of that room quick enough as my eyes were filling up with tears. I was so upset. Okay, so I did push the boundaries of rules and regulations, and some unfortunate circumstances had happened. But I was genuinely proud of wearing my uniform and took my work seriously, and I felt I did a bloody good job. I was and still am extremely patriotic. I wasn't the only one who enjoyed their social life with plenty of rule-breaking going on. Why me? I was deeply hurt by their decision and genuinely mortified to have this noted on my records. I truly felt this was totally unjustified and wondered why this decision had been made. Perhaps they thought I was capable of creating an embarrassing situation for the crown if serving abroad, like having an affair with a diplomat. How dare they? The more I thought about it, the more furious I became. I was beginning to think it was time I left Her Majesty's Senior Service even though I had another year to go.

Roy hadn't been idle whilst away and had made some good contacts, including Judy Kwaloff, who ran Windward Island Tours out of New Jersey. Apparently, she was a tough little lady who smoked cigars. She was willing to add Spirit of Cutty Sark to her list of yachts available for chartering. After a couple of weeks playing with figures and discussing what was needed, Roy and Leslie formed a partnership, and it was full steam ahead to get the boat ready for the transatlantic crossing and kitted out for chartering. One stipulation Roy made was that I would go along as cook/hostess, and although Leslie had some reservations, it was agreed. Basically, Leslie had no idea if I could cook; nor did I. Mum ruled the kitchen when I was living at home, and from then on I was fed by the navy. I did take domestic science as one of my GCEs, but that didn't prove anything. Was I capable of producing three-course meals for a bunch of American paying guests to a high standard?

There was also the problem of leaving the Wrens before my four years were up. I decided to apply for compassionate discharge although, as Roy and I were not married, I wasn't holding my breath. By this time it was the beginning of September. Whilst I was waiting for the decision I did some research, or more to the point a newly qualified solicitor friend did on my behalf. As the Wrens were not under the Naval Disciplinary Act but were governed by Wrens Standing Orders,

I would not be breaking any law by deserting. The only thing that might work against me is if I applied for a civil service job in the future.

All of a sudden timing had become of the essence. Leslie decided that it would be a good idea to enter Spirit of Cutty Sark in the Middle Seas Race which was hosted by Malta, the first of which had taken place the previous year. I believe the date was around the middle of October. Although I would not be involved in the racing, I would need to be in Malta by that time. Leslie had somehow managed to persuade the navy to supply the crew of his choice and have the boat shipped over rather than sail it round to the Med. As expected, my request for compassionate discharge was declined, and therefore I informed First Officer Wrens that I would be leaving at the beginning of October. I believe I was the only Wren on record at that time who had given notice of my intention to desert. One week later my awaited promotion to Leading Wren came through, backdated by one month. At first I was disinclined to accept the promotion. I was still smarting over not being allowed to go abroad and questioned why, in that case, were they obviously still trying to stop me leaving? When I muttered to Chief Wren Regulator that I was going to leave shortly so wouldn't bother taking up the promotion, she made it quite clear that I must accept it. I opted not to make any further fuss and therefore dutifully sewed on my Leading Wren badges to my uniforms. When I checked with a friend in the pay office to see if I would get my extra money that month, she informed me that they had strict instruction to hold this back for one month. I then found out that any money owing to you once you leave the Wrens goes to the Crown. Cheeky lot! When I told my lovely boss I was leaving, he patted my hand and said, 'Go. As a young sub-lieutenant I was down in the Grenadines doing survey work. I have always wanted to return to those beautiful islands. But

I ask you to do one thing. There is a postbox just outside the main gate. Would you please write a letter confirming you have left for good and pop it in the box as you leave? That way, I will get a replacement a lot quicker'. That was the least I could do for this wonderful, old-fashioned gentleman officer.

So, my next task was to tell my parents. My birthday was coming up on 19 September so I decided to go home that weekend on my own. My birthday was on the Friday. That morning I received one dozen red roses from Roy with a little note saying that he had taken out insurance to cover me to drive his car that weekend. He had a two-tone beige MGB GT. Wow! I was going home in style. My poor parents were to get yet another shock – in fact, two. Not only was I going to tell them their daughter was about to desert the Wrens, but that she would also be putting her life at risk by sailing across the Atlantic. Don't forget, in those days there was no satellite navigation, and communications were poor. If you needed help, you would be lucky if your SOS call was picked up by a passing ship, and then, of course, it would be a hard task finding you. The Atlantic is one hell of a big rolling ocean.

I waited until after supper, and once I had opened my cards and presents I dropped my bombshell. After a shocked silence my mother said, 'Oh my God!' Dad walked out of the room, but just as I began to get worried about his reaction he came back in and gave me a big hug, and said, 'Mum and I knew you were born under a wandering star. All I ask is that you take great care of yourself and let us know you're safe as soon as possible.' With all of us in tears I gave them both a big hug and told them how much I loved them. I then spent the rest of the weekend discussing various recipes with Mum and making piles of notes. She was a good home cook, particularly when it came to pastry and cakes, and her roast dinners were legendary. She was also an extremely practical woman, and for once in my life I took heed of all the advice she gave me.

At the first opportunity when I was back in Lee-on-Solent I bought some cookery books. I chose the two-paperback version of the Good Housekeeping's Cookery Encyclopaedia and Cooking for Compliments. These books became invaluable, and to this day I still use them. I decided that I needed a fool-proof week's menu, with some good backups should a charter be for longer than that. At Leslie's house, and at every opportunity, Roy and anyone else who was around were subjected to my experimental dishes, with me insisting on brutal feedback. As you can imagine, not every meal was a success, but I was quite chuffed and relieved to discover I did have some cooking skills and that they were improving at a good rate. I was also given the task of drawing up a list of kitchen equipment, tableware and linen that I reckoned would be required. It was a good job I took after my mum in the practical sense and thankfully, as I began to discover, was becoming quite a good organiser. The guys agreed to my suggestion of having bright orange Melaware plates and bowls with stainless steel serving dishes. That was typical of the sixties. Leslie put me in touch with a friend of one of his ladies who had done a little cooking on a yacht in the British Virgin Islands. I can't remember her name, but she gave me lots of very valuable advice which was desperately needed and appreciated. These days you would just google it!

Whilst I was concentrating on stocking the boat with all the equipment needed to transform the racing-mode interior to a more comfortable style that would appease our future American charterers, Roy was kept busy with the maintenance. He also adapted one of the quarter berths into a large icebox using thick sheets of foam. He divided the area in two. On one side he fitted four plastic boxes – two side by side, with a further two on top. The other side was left clear for the blocks of ice. This was going to be our only source of cold storage. For cooking, I had a calor gas gimballed stove consisting of two burners, a grill and a small oven.

In no time at all I found myself once again saying goodbye to Roy, but this time it was with great excitement. Along with the rest of the crew, Roy was going with Spirit of Cutty Sark on one of the merchant naval ships. By this time I had done the deed at work. I carefully laid out all my uniforms and kit on my folded-up bed and walked out with my head held high, posting the promised letter. I had no regrets, especially after knowing I would not be transferred anywhere overseas, which had been part of the reason for joining up in the first place. I was about to travel to far more exotic places and have the adventure of a lifetime, sailing across the Atlantic.

Chapter 6 – Sail Away

I spent a week at home with my parents and sisters, and said goodbye to some of my old schoolmates. Before I returned home, Mum was interviewed by the local gazette who did a small article about me as a local girl. It mentioned I had been in the navy and somewhat involved in the Torrey Canyon disaster, and that I was about to sail across the Atlantic. Fame at last! Dad made me laugh. He kept showing the article to everyone, proudly saying, 'That's my girl.'

Flying to Malta was my first experience of civilian air travel. I wasn't at all nervous, just incredibly excited. This was the start of a new phase of my life, and I felt so very lucky that I was about to do something that not many others had done. I stayed with a naval family who kindly put me up, which was something Leslie had arranged. The guy was one of the crew, chosen for his local knowledge. The whole week was a whirl of reception parties. As it was an international race week, each embassy hosted an evening of entertainment, along with a few of the large hotels, as a PR exercise. I definitely hadn't brought enough long dresses with me and had to go buy a couple more. Seeing the same people at each reception meant you had to be quite inventive with what you wore. It was all great fun, and at each party all the ladies were given a little gift. During the day whilst the racing was on I explored parts of the island, making use of the local buses. I was fascinated with Malta and loved its rugged coastline. It is a very staunch Roman Catholic country, and I found it interesting to see each person cross themselves on entering the bus. I loved the narrow streets full of old buildings, which surprised me. I had always thought of myself as a very modern girl and therefore assumed I would prefer the few more stylish areas in the centre of Valletta. I was amazed to find myself preferring to wander around some of the many old churches. This new revelation continued when it came to hotels. I developed a dislike for modern styles and to this day, whenever possible I choose to stay in a grand old building, even if it's slightly bent at the edges.

In addition to doing some sightseeing I also kept myself busy making lots of lists in preparation for catering for the crossing. Roger from The Jolly Roger was going to join us as our crew member for the season. He had just qualified as a pharmacist and wanted to take some time out.

Spirit of Cutty Sark took the trophy for the overall winning yacht. How brilliant was that? The celebrations went on long into the night. The following day, with massive hangovers, the boat was cleaned up and made ready for sea, including buying and storing away enough provisions for the first leg to Gibraltar. By then Roger had joined us, complete with a fully equipped first aid kit. On 15 November 1969 we set sail. In addition to Roy, Roger and me, there were also quite a few naval chaps from the aircraft carrier HMS Eagle. The arrangement was that they would rejoin their ship once we reached Gib. I had such a mixture of emotions. I was nervous and apprehensive but also full of excitement. Up till then my longest sail was from Cherbourg to Alderney and then back to Portsmouth. It was estimated that the leg to Gibraltar would take around six to nine days depending on the weather. Would I be able to cope okay? I was the least experienced on board and certainly the youngest. I just had to prove to them all that I was not a silly young girl, and I was determined not to let Roy down. In his usual laid-back way Roy had not uttered one word of doubt, which helped a lot to qualm my nerves.

In total there were ten of us, with me being the only female. As I was doing the cooking, I was excluded from watch duty which was great news as I got to sleep through the night. The nine were split into three watches and were named Haig, Teachers and Bells. What a great bunch of guys, most of them very experienced sailors. Included in the crew was Dickie Bird who, at one stage during his naval career, was the Queen's coxswain on the royal yacht Britannia. He also used to sail on Bloodhound, a racing yacht owned by the royal family. It was on this yacht that the Queen and Duke's children learnt to sail, and Dickie told us a lovely story of how Princess Anne would happily dish out corned beef sandwiches to the crew which she had made herself down in the galley. Another story concerned when he was serving on Britannia during one Cowes Week. Prince Edward had been pestering his parents to be allowed to sail one of the dinghies. Eventually the Duke ordered Dickie to take him sailing and remain out with him for two whole hours. This he dutifully did, even though Prince Edward wanted to return a lot earlier.

Tugg Wilson was another member of the crew. Apart from serving in the Fleet Air Arm he was also a brilliant and well-loved cartoonist for naval publications, and later worked for the Daily Mirror. He had a great sense of humour and certainly kept our spirits up over the seven days it took to sail to Gib, which included some rough weather sailing. Just before leaving us Tugg got out his sketch book and quickly drew three great cartoons which summed up the trip in a wonderful, funny way. Such a talented guy. Sadly, one of the sketches got damaged, although I still have it. The other two I have hung at home in our guest bathroom, and each time I look at them memories of this time come flooding back.

Alarmingly and disappointingly, I discovered I suffered from sea sickness, which had not happened on previous weekend trips. It only lasted for the first forty-eight hours, after which I was fine in all weather conditions. Thankfully, and with great relief, it didn't knock me out. I would be down below in the galley and suddenly would have to rush up on deck to throw up. I would then be fine for another couple of hours or so before rushing up again. From then onwards this would happen on every new boat I sailed – each time just for the first forty-eight hours. Once I got over my seasickness I was able to relax more, and I started to enjoy the sailing, although most of the time it was wet and a little too windy, causing quite an uncomfortable lumpy sea. I successfully kept the crew fed and began to feel I was now part of the team. Although it was tough going, I had not let Roy down. Phew!

Unfortunately, about halfway to Gib, I developed a boil at the bottom of my spine which was not only painful but very embarrassing. As you can imagine, there was much joking about it, but also some sympathy. So much so that on arriving in Gib, one of the crew, a young sub lieutenant, rushed ashore and arranged for me to have a hot bath over at the Wren officers' mess. Feeling really chuffed, he was therefore surprised to be met with sheer panic in my face when he told me what he had done. When I explained the reason why, he was mortified that he had put me in such a potentially difficult situation. After a lot of discussion, everyone felt that I should still go along. It was quite a long shot that I would meet anyone who knew me or the fact I had recently deserted. I was more than a little nervous when I entered the officers' mess and jumped every time someone new entered the room. They ran me a hot steaming bath filled with perfumed salts and plonked a large glass of white wine in my hand. I was in heaven, and the soak did the trick. With great relief the boil burst, and I didn't bump into anyone who knew me. Fortunately, one of their friends was being a DJ on the base's radio station for the first time, so the main focus was listening to the programme and I was spared any awkward questions. I was extremely grateful to those girls for their kindness. The next few days were spent frantically working through a list an arm long of maintenance items and stocking up the boat with enough provisions to take us across the Atlantic. Although we would also be stopping in Tenerife it was easier to get everything in Gib, it being a British port. All I would then need to get in Tenerife would be the fresh produce. I had been told there was a brilliant market there.

Our lovely naval crew members had already rejoined HMS Eagle, which left just the three of us until a couple from London arrived – James and Amelia. They were 'paid' guests which Leslie had arranged. Roy was not too pleased as it meant we would be taking two people who we had not met beforehand. He wasn't bothered about them being inexperienced. Being an ex-sail training officer, he was used to that. What was more important was whether they would fit in with the three of us. It wasn't as if it was a week or two of chartering. We would be living close together for some weeks at sea. You couldn't exactly leave the boat for a break in the middle of the Atlantic! They joined us the day before we were due to leave. I had already formed a picture in my mind and was quite amazed that James and Amelia were just as I imagined. They were both quite tall and very much part of the London set, immaculately dressed in their designer clothes, and we would hear plenty of 'yah's which made Roy and I giggle. My first thought was how on earth was Amelia going to keep her beautiful long hair so well maintained during the crossing, and I made a mental note to remind Roy to point out to them how precious fresh water would be during the weeks ahead.

On 30 November 1969, eight days after arriving, we left Gib. I never had a chance to see much of this famous naval port as we were all kept busy preparing for our next leg. This time I wasn't so nervous and felt confident I could cope. I was therefore a lot more at ease when we set off. As soon as Roy set the course to Tenerife, we immediately had to put four rolls in the mainsail due to thirty-five knots of wind. Despite the large rollers we made good progress. Within twenty-four hours the wind had dropped to eight knots, creating an uncomfortable wallowing motion. I was relieved to discover my stomach remained firm, although Amelia had definitely lost her appetite – sorry, no smoked salmon bagels or Italian breads on board. We had given James and Amelia the forward cabin, but after the first day they opted to sleep in the lounge. The following day, when Roy needed something that was stored under one of the forward bunks, he discovered that Amelia had been sick all over one of the new light crochet blankets, hadn't told us and just left it up forward with the door firmly closed. What a stink. That poor blanket was trailed behind the boat for some hours before it was allowed back on board. On day two, the loo became blocked. Poor Roy had the unpleasant job of emptying and dismantling it in order to clear it. The joys of being at sea.

I discovered a great love of the ocean and was not at all fazed by knowing land was many miles away. I found great peace when surrounded by nothing but a vast expanse of water. I particularly enjoyed doing the dawn watch. With everyone else asleep I loved being alone in the cockpit, relishing the sound of the wind in the sails and the whooshing sound of the bow slicing through the waves. What power being in control of a 53ft racing yacht that responded so well to my touch on the steering wheel. Watching the sun rise on the horizon and gradually light up the surrounding sea is a memory that I will always treasure; the start of a new day of what was becoming an amazing experience.

Three days later, on 3 November at 0150, we arrived in Tenerife. I experienced such a great thrill in arriving at our destination. I get this great kick of excitable anticipation and can't wait to get ashore. This constant desire to explore new places has never left me. Coming into the harbour I was surprised to discover how much of the land I could smell. It was a mixture of many different things, making it rather sweet and earthy. I'm guessing breathing such clear air at sea for some days must sharpen your senses.

We managed to find a mooring, hoisted our 'Q' flag and collapsed on our bunks for a well-earned few hours' sleep. A plain yellow flag stands for 'Q' and in old terms means 'quarantine', but in modern terms it means the vessel is free of disease and requires custom and immigration clearance. Until this is done no one is allowed ashore. For that reason you often have to anchor out and wait for the officers to come to you by boat. Once cleared the following morning we were able to tie up alongside the harbour wall just down from the yacht club. Spanish yacht clubs are renowned for being very snobby and exclusive, except for the one in Tenerife. Visiting yachts are made welcome and are allowed to use their facilities, and can also use the club as a mailing address. I believe this is because most visiting are serious long-distance sailors and therefore earn a good deal of respect. When sailing from Europe to the West Indies or further, most would leave at about the same time as we did, hopefully ahead of the nasty winter depressions, and then wait it out in the Canary Islands until the trade winds kicked in, which is normally between December and January. You could either flog it to windward going miles out of your way, or you could wait patiently in the comfort of a good, sheltered harbour and, once they arrive, allow the trade winds to blow you roughly in the direction you want to go. It's a no-brainer.

To be quite honest I was expecting our guests to jump ship once we arrived in Tenerife. Well, at least Amelia. Apart from being seasick, the three days we were at sea she spent most of the time below decks complaining it wasn't warm enough. James definitely enjoyed it a lot more and I have the feeling he persuaded her to stick it out. Once we were able to get ashore we saw very little of them. They headed straight to a hotel and remained there until we left the island – most likely a condition laid down by Amelia.

I loved our time in Tenerife. In between working on the boat we took some time off to do a little sightseeing, something I was constantly badgering Roy to do. This was my first real experience of a foreign place where English was not the main language. Hiring a small car, Roy, Roger and I set off for the day to explore the island. We decided to head up towards the top of Mount Teide. Not only was this the highest mountain on the island but the highest in the whole of Spain. We started off in somewhat tropical terrain. Once away from the port of Santa Cruz I was thrilled to see plenty of palm trees and became really excited at seeing my first banana tree. Wow! The next surprise I got was seeing a herd of camels. This made me realise we were not that far from Africa. As we continued to climb, the landscape changed. More and more trees appeared, and before we knew it we found ourselves driving along the edge of a pine forest. Further up, the trees started to thin out until all that was left was barren rock with hardly a blade of grass to be seen. It was at this point our little car started to splutter and then stopped. It had literally run out of air. When we got out of the car I was shocked to discover how much colder it had become, and I found it harder to breathe. It was incredible to experience such a contrast in weather and terrain in just a few hours of driving. The top of the mountain was still a little distance away. A cable car lead to the very top which was shrouded in cloud, but we decided not to walk the short distance up to it. Apart from anything else we hadn't come prepared for such a drop in temperature. On the way back down we stopped at a little café where I couldn't resist ordering garlic soup for lunch. It was delicious. Driving along the coastline back towards Santa Cruz I had another surprise. Seeing a row of palm trees, I was expecting a beach of golden sand. Instead, it was black. Roy explained that as the island was volcanic, the sand was made from tiny fragments of lava. I found this really weird and insisted that we stop so I could run my fingers through it. The people on the island were so friendly, and back in Santa Cruz there were brightly coloured flowers everywhere.

Santa Cruz harbour was beginning to fill up with quite a number of yachts all waiting to cross the big pond. Roy was a great socialiser, so it wasn't long before we got to know everyone, and there were many evening gatherings on various yachts. On one particular night we played host, and what a great evening it turned out to be. Someone brought along a guitar, and aided with many a jug of gin and 'pusser's' lime juice it became quite a lively affair. Pusser's (a word for naval) lime juice, by the way, was a very concentrated lime powder that was mixed with water to make a wonderful lime squash. We had acquired quite a few tins of this. In amongst all the revelry I noticed an older chap sitting quietly in the corner. When I asked him which yacht he was on, he replied that he wasn't on one but had a wooden rowing boat. He was a large man in his fifties with a broad Midlands accent. I asked where exactly he had rowed from. Expecting him to say from somewhere around the coast, I was astounded to hear him say Cornwall. After I repeated this to make sure I had heard correctly, the cabin fell silent for a few seconds, then everyone started to speak at once, firing off all sorts of questions. As he explained himself in a very matter-of-fact way, I noticed how huge his hands were. His name was Sid Genders and he was rowing from England to Florida singlehanded. He was held up in Tenerife due to not receiving his next supply of dried food. This was supposed to have been supplied by Horlicks Company, but in between him leaving England and arriving in the Canary Islands, Horlicks had been taken over by the Beecham Group, and his agreed supply had not arrived. As he was having difficulty trying to get hold of the right person to sort it out, Roy contacted the Cutty Sark whisky PR people who then promised to help out.

Many months later we heard that Sid did get his food supply and, although he wasn't destined to do so, made a stop in Antigua en route to Florida. He had already passed the island when his final freshwater container burst. He then had to row against the trade winds back to Antigua to replenish his supply. Whilst there, he apparently met a lovely American lady who was then waiting for him when he finally made it to Florida. What an amazing man, and what an incredible thing to achieve. It made our sailing across the Atlantic to the West Indies in a comfortable yacht, complete with navigational aids and good cooking facilities, an absolute doddle. There is a lovely end to this story. Being a divorcee, Sid ended up marrying the lovely American lady, who had plenty of money, and they lived happily ever after in comfort. At least, I sincerely hope he did.

All of a sudden, there was a flurry of activity; the weather indicated that the trade winds had arrived. It was time to hit the market and buy the fresh produce needed for the crossing. I had already checked it out and was not disappointed with what I found. With my Spanish dictionary in one hand and my list in the other, off I went. It was a large covered area, bustling with people and noise. The centre was full of stalls selling fresh fruit, vegetables and flowers. Around the perimeter were the fresh meat, cheese and cold meat suppliers. Buying the fruit and veg was no problem. The stallholders gave me plastic bags for me to help myself. I just had to trust they were being honest, which my gut feeling told me they were. Cheese and cold meats were also easy. I simply pointed and expanded my hands to roughly the size I wanted, and did a chopping motion with my hand if I wanted something sliced. However, fresh meat was a challenge as virtually none of it was on display. Behind the counter was the butcher with a chopping board, with everything stored in large coolers behind him. I lost patience with the dictionary and decided miming was the way forward. I snorted, mooed and baa-baaed my way through the list of what I needed. Lamb's liver and pork chops were the hardest to communicate. It was hysterical, and by the time I'd finished I had collected a large crowd of people, some of whom had tears of laughter running down their faces. After weighing each lot, the butcher kept adding extra as a thank you for giving him so much entertainment and attracting more customers. I came away exhausted but chuffed to bits at having managed to get everything on the list. I felt quite proud of my efforts.

We alerted James and Amelia, who returned to the boat looking a few shades browner and distinctly refreshed. There were lots of fond farewells and good wishes – particularly to Sid – and on 9 December we left Tenerife, our next destination being Bequia, the island where Roy had worked the previous year, which was to become our base in the Windward Islands. To begin with the wind was a steady eight knots, but it soon became very light. The trade winds hadn't properly settled in, but after a couple of days they returned. The spinnaker was hoisted and we started to make good progress.

In 1969 there was no satellite navigation. Back then, a sextant was used. It was essential that you had accurate time, and that you log your distance and speed over water, and the course you are heading, which gives you your latitude – known as DR (dead reckoning). The easiest way to check that you are where you think you are is to do a noon sun sight. With the use of the sextant you measure the distance from the sun to the horizon when the sun is at its highest point. To make it a lot easier, tables (known as sight reduction tables) have been devised from a number of different sources. Reeds were the most common ones used then by the British, but Roy opted to use the naval version which came with a form to guide you through the calculations, along with a plotting sheet. For accurate time we had a Rolex clock mounted on a gimbal, carefully stored in a wooden box. All this worked fine, as long as you saw the sun; and in rough weather this was often not the case. If there was a big swell, it could be a challenge getting an accurate reading of the horizon whilst trying to keep the sextant and yourself steady on a rolling deck. Roughly halfway across the Atlantic we were able to pick up the time clock from Jacksonville, Florida, on the two-way radio, which was a great help in making sure the timing instrument was correct.

We soon got into a steady routine. I opted for my favourite dawn watch which suited everyone else. We had a self-steering wind vane which we called Fred. It was quite temperamental, and Roy spent many hours fiddling and repairing it. We had to watch it when running downwind as it would suddenly veer off, causing mayhem with the spinnaker. Every other day I made two loaves of bread. I would do this during my dawn watch so the rest of the crew would wake up with the smell of freshly baked bread. I rationed us to one loaf a day, so had to hide the second one as it was far too tempting if left in sight.

Every now and again a squall would hit us. Running with the wind meant that they would sneak up from the stern. Whoever was on watch therefore had to constantly look behind to see if any big black clouds started to gather. As soon as this happened the alarm was raised. This caused a flurry of activity as the spinnaker needed to be dropped before the wind caught up with us. Once the deck was cleared, we would grab some soap and shampoo with the hope of getting enough rain to have a decent freshwater shower. When the rain hit the mainsail it would pour down along the boom and run towards the mast, creating an excellent stream of water to stand under. Most of the time it rained for long enough to get a good rinsing off after lathering up, but this was not always the case. On a number of occasions we ended up finishing off with buckets of salt water, which rather defeated the exercise.

Fresh water was very precious and we had to use it sparingly. I discovered potatoes and vegetables could be cooked in salt water, but pasta absorbed too much salt. All the washing-up was done in a bucket of salt water in the cockpit. Amelia had great difficulty in adapting to life on a boat. For some benign reason she wore make-up every day. This meant she used wads of toilet paper to clean it off. At the rate she was doing this I knew we would run out of toilet rolls long before we reached Bequia. She also managed to block the toilet once again by putting too much paper down it. The third time Roy had to dismantle it he found the offending item was a tampon. As it had been clearly explained to her beforehand not to put them down the loo, he was so mad he waved the offending item in front of everyone, including Amelia, and said if it happened again, she would be the one to unblock it. From then onwards Amelia made quite a point of publicly dumping her tampons overboard, and thankfully the loo never got blocked again.

We had an electric water pump so a tap could be run in the head (bathroom). A mug of water was quite ample for brushing your teeth. But not for Amelia! Every time she was in the head

Roy and I would wince at the length of time the water pump ran for. Sure enough, the water tank was emptying far too quickly, so in the finish Roy had to turn the pump off. From then onwards the only way to get any fresh water was to use the foot pump in the galley, which was not so easy and was in full sight of everyone.

We would rarely see another vessel once out of the main shipping lanes, and even more rarely another yacht. It was therefore quite a surprise when on watch I shouted out, 'Sail to starboard.' Roy thought I was kidding. But sure enough, there she was. We altered course to get closer and made a note in the log that it was Que Vive. It was quite a small yacht, sailing very slowly under a short rig. They indicated that they were okay, and we made signs to switch on the radio. We tried calling them but with no luck. We next saw them when they finally arrived in the Grenadines many weeks after us. It was customary in those days, and I do hope that it is still the case, for all ships to check any yacht seen and log the sighting and position.

In the middle of the Atlantic there was no pollution, and on a clear night the stars and planets were so vivid that they gave the impression of being much closer to Earth. If the self-steering was working, I would get up on top of the coach roof, lie flat on my back and stare up above. Lying there, feeling the warm breeze and listening to the sound of the boat running with the big Atlantic rollers, I would stare up at the millions of stars within such a clear velvet-blue sky. It was as though I could just raise my hand and touch them. It was pure magic. I kept shaking my head in disbelief of where I was. I couldn't say I was living a dream; never in my wildest thoughts as a young teenager did I ever think I would be where I was now, and be able to sail such an amazingly fast and powerful yacht in the middle of the Atlantic. I still feel very privileged and fortunate that I had that experience, and I will always treasure those very special memories.

Once we had left Tenerife and land behind, dolphins often came to visit us and would keep us company for long periods of time. On one occasion I almost jumped out of my skin when I was alone on the dawn watch. It was just beginning to get light, and for once Fred was behaving himself, so I was totally relaxed, sitting in the cockpit having a cigarette. Suddenly a loud whooshing sound came from alongside the hull. A whale had come to the surface. He was so close. He had come to check us out. I sat there mesmerised, his eye staring right at me as if trying to communicate – it was so eerie. I was fascinated with the amount of barnacles on his back as I watched his huge grey body slowly disappear, with some relief. What if it had hit us – would it have damaged the hull?

Another thing happened whilst on my watch which was quite disturbing. We had the spinnaker up and all was going well. Suddenly one end of the sail somehow managed to unhook itself, and before I knew it we were broached, which means the boat was virtually on its side. I had all my weight on the wheel, but no way could I bring the nose round. I screamed for Roy. He knew instantly what had happened, as he found himself walking on the side of the boat when he climbed out of his bunk. He shouted to me to let both spinnaker sheets fly, whilst with the aid of the engine he managed to bring the boat round to windward. By then the rest of the crew were up, and there was frantic pulling on the mainsail sheet to stop the boom thrashing about. We then had to retrieve the spinnaker from the sea and unravel all the ropes. It was quite a scary time, and what a rude awakening to the day!

Some things that I learnt about cooking at sea:

• On good advice I bought a pressure cooker. Not only did this save a lot of gas usage, but being such a deep pot it was ideal in rough weather. No fear of soup being slopped out.

• Do not make treacle tart in a rolling sea. There is only so much a gimbal stove can manage, and as it swung back and forth, the treacle slopped out of the tart, landing on the gas burner at the back of the oven. It took me days to scrape off all the sticky mess; and what a stink every time I turned on the oven.

• Another bit of good advice: cover eggs with Vaseline. This stops air getting through the shells, which prolongs the life of the eggs. Even near the end of the trip, by then in tropical weather, only a few of those left had gone bad, and that was probably because they hadn't been completely covered.

• Always be prepared for the occasional lurch from an extra big wave. It took three attempts to make a lemon meringue pie. Whilst I was making the filling, the cooked tart base shot across the galley and shattered all over the navigation table. Second attempt: one filled tart minus meringue upended itself into the bin below. At least there was no mopping up. I refused to be beaten; the third attempt was completed and enjoyed by all.

On 21 December, Barbados was sighted bang on target. Well done, Roy, with the navigation. We were now getting very excited as our destination, Bequia, was only a few days away. By 2300 on Christmas Eve we were sailing up the east side of Bequia. The spinnaker had been dropped and we were heading close into the wind. I had baked a batch of mince pies earlier that day. With the warm spray hitting our faces, there we were, singing Christmas carols at the top of our voices and munching somewhat soggy mince pies. That is, except for Amelia. She was sleeping below and did not wish to be up at that hour. She came to experience the excitement of such a trip, yet chose to miss such a momentous part of it. We finally dropped anchor in Admiralty Bay, Bequia, at 0200 on Christmas Day. Wow, what an amazing Christmas present. After toasting the success of the trip with a hefty glass of Cutty Sark whisky, we all collapsed for a few hours of sleep. I just couldn't wait to see the island in daylight.

Chapter 7 – The Grenadines

I awoke with the sun in my eyes. I had crashed out in the cockpit where Roy had left me covered with a blanket. It took a few seconds for me to register that the boat wasn't moving, and then, joy oh joy, I remembered we had arrived. I jumped up and stared around me. It was so beautiful. We were anchored just off the small Frangipani Bar and Hotel. The scene was straight out of a luxury holiday brochure – white sand, turquoise water and many palm trees. I cried with the sheer wonder of it all; unbelievably, I was living the dream of how I imagined the island would be. I did no more than dive overboard and swim ashore. I simply had to dig my toes into that soft white sand.

By the time I got back to the boat the rest of the crew had started to emerge. A quick breakfast used up the last of the eggs, and by 0900 we were alongside Bequia slip. With no thanks to Amelia, we had almost run out of water but were able to get a little to tide us over before reaching St Vincent, where we would be able to properly fill our tank. It was just as well we made such a quick crossing: just fourteen and a half days from Tenerife to Bequia. We had broken the record, and this was to remain so for some years. As soon as we were tied up, Amelia made a beeline for dry land. She had spotted a hose at the end of the jetty, and in no time at all she was using it to wash her hair. Unfortunately, we hadn't noticed what she was doing until the manager, Tim Burgess, shouted at her to stop in a very distraught manner. Bequia does not have any natural springs so the only source of fresh water is from water catchments that collect and store rainwater. She was using his own private source. In the time it took to stop her she had drained half of Tim's tank. Not good news for someone with a wife and four children. She really was something else.

Later that day we took a taxi over to Friendship Bay where Roy had worked the previous year. There I met two brothers, Ron and Stan Young. Ron managed the hotel and Stan did the charters on their own Gallant 53s. Sitting there, being cooled by the warm trade wind, enjoying my first rum punch whilst listening to the sound of the waves softly lapping the beach, was heavenly. It was here that I first tasted the wonderful food of the West Indies. What a way to end a very special Christmas Day.

By 1000 the following day we slipped our anchor and sailed the two hours over to St Vincent, where Amelia and James disembarked. Roger, Roy and I all breathed a sigh of relief once they left. We got on just about, but they really were not our sort of people; especially Amelia, who was rather hard work. We heard later that they got married, so at least their relationship survived the crossing.

Leaving Roy and Roger to sort out refuelling with both diesel and water, I set off for the market which was close by. I stood there taking in the vibrant and exotic atmosphere full of noise and bustle. There was a lot of shouting from men wheeling wooden barrows in between stallholders shouting their wares, all competing with loud reggae music. The women wore such bright colours, and I was fascinated to watch how they carried their produce on top of their heads. There was so much laughter, and big smiles on many faces. Each wooden stall was overflowing with fruit and vegetables, some of which I didn't recognise. And bananas; there were so many for sale everywhere I looked, and the air was full of their sweet smell. I was totally entranced. In no time at all I returned laden with lots of fresh goodies, accompanied by a young boy carrying a stem of bananas. Roy had instructed me to buy it – they had to be green ones. Apparently, you tied them at the back of the boat and worked through eating them as they become ripe. Before bringing the bananas on board, the whole stem was dunked in the water and held there for a minute or so. This was to make sure no unwelcome visitors joined us. Cockroaches and scorpions were the favourites. By then Cutty Sark's tanks were full, and her decks were gleaming from having a good scrub down. We then walked over to Hazel's supermarket where we met Jeff and Dick Gunn for the first time. They were tall, slender and very pale white twin brothers, and came from an old established colonial Vincentian family. I loved their accent which was vaguely reminiscent of the soft sing-song Welsh voice. Yet more food was stored on board. The spirit mixers came in small bottles in wooden crates. These too were dunked under water before being allowed on board. The boat was now well stocked with masses of food and drink. Jeff and Dick warned us, as the island heavily depended on imports, to make sure to buy plenty of what we needed when we saw it as there was no guarantee it would be in stock all the time. This proved to be excellent advice.

Once we completed all our tasks, we headed off to the Cobblestone Inn where we met the owners – an English couple, Martin and Caroline. Little did I know that I would appreciate their generosity so much the following year. The inn was situated right in the centre of Kingstown and it had air conditioning. It became our favourite haunt for lunch when in town. A fresh lime squash or cold beer with a toasted ham and cheese sandwich was the favourite. That afternoon we moved the boat over to Young Island, where we anchored. Young Island is an exclusive private hotel complex just two hundred yards off the southern end of St Vincent. It was owned by an American businessman and managed by his daughter Julie and her English husband, Simon, who used to be one of the yacht skippers chartering in the area. That night we went ashore and met them for drinks. Roy was keen to make them aware we were available for charters – day trips to Mustique, or longer trips further down the Grenadines. It was a lovely social evening and it was where I discovered my absolute favourite drink – banana daiquiri. As they took so long to make, from then onwards Roy would groan every time I ordered one and plead with the bartender to bring his beer first.

On 27 December we left to return to our base at Bequia but sailed via Mustique. For those who don't know, it is a very exclusive private island eighteen miles south of St Vincent. At that time it was owned by Colin Tennant, who later became Lord Glenconner. He had given his close friend Princess Margaret a sizable plot as a wedding present when she married Lord Snowdon in 1960. At the time we were there, Colin was only just beginning to develop the island. The old cotton warehouse hotel conversion had yet to be completed, along with the airstrip, Princess Margaret's house was still in design stage, and the infamous Basil's Bar was still only an idea in Colin's head. As soon as her house was built Princess Margaret spent a great deal of time there and often hosted parties, inviting many of the yachting fraternity who happened to be around. Unfortunately, we were never there at the right time to attend any, although many others we knew did. Apparently, on one occasion her husband Lord Snowdon decided to pay a visit, but when he arrived in Barbados permission was not granted for him to continue on to Mustique. It was the start of a troublesome time for them!

The next few days were spent getting the boat in tip-top condition for chartering, and we caught up on our letter writing. Making a phone call in the West Indies was not easy, so it was by letter that Mum and Dad heard of my safe arrival, which was well into January. Thinking back they must have been quite worried over Christmas, but they never let on and never made me feel guilty. I now have grown-up kids and worry if they don't call me after only a couple of hours of travelling back home after visiting us. What I put my parents through doesn't bear thinking about.

The Frangipani Bar and small hotel became our favourite watering hole ashore in Bequia. It was covered with bougainvillea, and lots of colourful hibiscus bushes were scattered around, along with the very fragrant frangipani. I liked nothing better than to lie on one of the loungers with a rum drink in hand, watching the spectacular sunset, inhaling the heavenly smells of the blossoms that surrounded me, and listening to the gentle lapping of water. It was the perfect tonic at the end of a busy day. The Frangi was managed by Maria, a Canadian lady who came on a visit and never left. It was owned by quite a dominant political figure – James Fitz-Allen Mitchell, who was known as Son Mitchell. At that time he was very active with the Labour Party, becoming Premier in 1972 and then Prime Minister in the eighties after St Vincent and the Grenadines gained independence in 1979. He was knighted by the Queen in 1995 for services to his country. His autobiography Beyond the Islands makes for interesting reading.

On 2 January we were back in Kingstown, stocking the boat up for our first charter – a week down the Grenadines with Bob and Eleanor Harris and their teenage son Guy. We got on so well with them that for years afterwards we kept in touch, and we stayed with them in New Jersey when we were in the US. From then onwards, thanks to Judy Kwaloff, Young Island, Friendship Bay Hotel and Tim Burgess at Bequia Slip, we were kept busy throughout the season. It was mostly back and forth in the Grenadines, but occasionally a charter would take us to St Lucia and Martinique. I had a set menu, and with a few adjustments it worked well. As I got to know what to do with them, I started to introduce some of the local produce like plantain (a cooking banana), christophine, which belongs to the squash family, and paw paw, better known as papaya. The islands still depended heavily on imported foods, and at one stage we couldn't get any potatoes – thank goodness for rice and instant mash! Fresh milk was non-existent, but UHT milk had just been introduced which was great news. Because cold storage was still a challenge out there, a lot of things came in tins, including butter, which helped with our own cold storage restrictions on board. The icebox that Roy made back in England worked well so long as it was only opened once a day. We had a couple of large igloos with blocks of ice – one for drinks, the other for the day's supply of food – which I would transfer from the icebox first thing in the morning. We always trailed two fishing lines. Nothing fancy; we just used thick line and double hooks with bright yellow feathers as lures. The lines were fastened round a cleat on each side of the boat, with some slack running through a tied-on peg attached to a stanchion. When they pinged, we had a bite and we used a winch to bring the catch in. Most of the time we would end up having a good fish at some stage during the week, which made for an excellent meal. Often it would be a dolphin – not the lovely porpoise type; this was a greeny-yellow fish with a large, ugly head. Known as dorado or mahi mahi in other parts of the world, it's the best-tasting fish ever – especially if cooked on the day it's caught. Kingfish was another good option that we sometimes caught.

The Grenadines are the most beautiful group of small islands between St Vincent and Grenada. Some, like Palm Island and Petit St Vincent, along with of course Mustique, are privately owned and are exclusive hotels. The good news is that visiting yachts are always welcome and each one is happy to accommodate your charterers for lunch or dinner should they choose to dip into their pockets to pay for it. This didn't happen often as each charter was all-inclusive including drinks. However, when our guests did decide to do so it gave me an unexpected, pleasurable break.

Within the Grenadines is a very small group of uninhabited islands called Tobago Cays. They are surrounded by coral reefs making it an excellent place for snorkelling. Local boys from nearby Union Island would spend their days there diving for lobster to sell to the visiting yachts. They still do to this day. They would cook them for you on the beach in old biscuit tins and bring them out to you. Little palm-fringed islands with white sand surrounded by the lightest of turquoise-coloured water, they are breathtakingly beautiful. Two dogs lived on one of them. Some cruel person must have dumped them there. Over time they became quite wild, keeping well away from people. It became a habit for all visiting boats to leave scraps and bones and some fresh water for them. We would see them watching from a small rise, and they would only come down to the beach once we had left in the dinghy. By the end of the first year only one dog remained. The island was always referred to as Dog Island.

Close to Tobago Cays is Palm Island. It used to be called Prune Island before John and Mary Caldwell bought it from the St Vincent government in 1966, on a 99-year lease for very little money. John had a vision of converting the uninhabited swampy nothingness into a luxury hotel complex. The very nominal price paid was on the proviso he employed a number of local people from nearby Union Island. Prior to acquiring Palm Island he was known as Coconut Johnny. He and Mary, with their two little boys, used to charter out of Antigua, and whenever the opportunity arose, John would plant coconut saplings wherever he went throughout the islands. At the end of the Second World War, being stuck in Panama and wanting to get back to Australia to join his darling wife, Mary, as a very novice sailor John bought a small boat and attempted to sail to Australia. He wrote a book titled Desperate Voyage which tells of his incredible journey on which he eventually became shipwrecked and very nearly died. Roy had brought back a signed copy of the book the previous year, and I had read it during our crossing. I couldn't wait to meet him and Mary, and what a fascinating couple they were. Whilst Mary was a wonderful, calm lady, John was never still. He had an enormous amount of energy, and what he managed to achieve on the island was incredible. It was like a nature reserve with small bungalows built to blend in, with a central bar and restaurant area. So many bright tropical flowers everywhere, and lots of birds. It was there that I saw my first hummingbird.

I also met their eldest son, Johnny, who was in charge of their launch which brought the guests over from Union Island. Their other son, Roger, was still at college back in America. John also helped to preserve the local turtle population which was slowly but surely disappearing. This was due to two things. Anything made in turtleshell was very popular in the sixties, and secondly, the West Indians regarded turtle eggs as a strong aphrodisiac. They would wait until the female turtles came up the beach to lay their eggs at night, and catch them before they returned to the sea. All they had to do was turn them over to rot in the sun, and dig up the eggs. So cruel. With John's influence, the government put prohibition signs up on the beaches, and once the eggs hatched, John would catch as many of the young turtles as possible and put them in a pool especially built at Palm Island. He would then release them once they were bigger in order to raise the survival rate. I have since learnt that John, at the age of eighty, died of a heart attack on his beloved island, and Mary has written her own book about their sailing days entitled Mary's Voyage, sixty years after Desperate Voyage was written. A brave lady herself, she not only recalls all their challenges at sea with a young family, but also describes all the hard work that went into achieving John's vision.

There were not many places in the Grenadines where you could re-provision, but at Union Island you could get blocks of ice, fresh bread, and some fresh veg and fruit. You really had to try and get most of what you needed in St Vincent before setting off. Most of the islands in the Grenadines belonged to St Vincent, but the two islands of Carriacou and Petit St Vincent belonged to Grenada. The advice that was always given by agents and ourselves was to start your sailing trip in St Vincent and disembark at Grenada. This meant that most of the sailing would be on a broad reach, which would certainly keep your rum punches steady. With short, steep seas, flogging to windward to get back to St Vincent could be very unpleasant. Entering one country from another involves customs and immigration, and the Grenadines are no exception. Boats therefore tended to clear out from Union Island and clear in at Carriacou. In those days the paperwork was very tedious and time-consuming. That is, unless a bottle of scotch was handed over.

Petit St Vincent was another exclusive private island. The story goes that a rich American asked two of the charter yacht skippers, Haze Richardson and Doug Terman, to go find him an island. This they did in 1962. At that time it was owned by a lady who lived in neighbouring Petit Martinique, and although it was thought she would never sell, she succumbed to the charms of both guys and a deal was agreed. Like John Caldwell, Haze and Doug worked hard transforming it into another beautiful luxury hotel complex. The first thing they had to do was build a desalination plant as there was no fresh water on the island. For months Haze and Doug lived on their schooner, Jacinta, whilst the building work continued. Haze ended up as manager whilst Doug continued chartering Jacinta. I had already met Doug back in St Vincent, and once I had met Haze I could well understand how the lady succumbed to selling the island. Haze ended up owning the island but sadly died in a freak swimming accident in Costa Rica in 2008. Petit St Vincent, affectionately known as PSV, was a great favourite of the charter fleet. 'Jump Up', a West Indian name for a party, complete with a steel band, was a weekly event there. It took place on a Thursday, and, if possible, we would work our charter to be there for that night. It was a great opportunity to catch up with everyone, and what a fun way to do it. PSV tended to be our last stop before reaching Grenada and was usually at the end of the charter, and then we would hightail it back to St Vincent to prepare for the next one.

When we were really busy this meant that the next one was the following day. The morning would be spent stripping and changing bed linen, cleaning the boat inside and out, and then rushing around St Vincent buying up the provisions, ice and so on needed for the next trip. We would meet at the Cobblestones for a late lunch, exhausted and dripping wet with perspiration, gasping for a cold beer, and relishing the air conditioning. The favourite expression of the day was 'another shitty day in paradise'. By the time the taxi arrived with the new batch of guests, we would be freshly showered and neatly dressed with a big smile on our faces. Where did all that energy come from? Quite often they would be very pale, tired and stressed out, and hit us with a million and one anxious questions. We would do no more than sit them in the cockpit, stow the bags below and set sail. The timing was such that whilst sipping their first rum punch (always an extra strong one) they would enjoy an easy sail, watching the sun set, and have their first supper anchored in Admiralty Bay in the beautiful island of Bequia. You could literally see the stress lines on their faces slowly disappear.

At the end of the season the Bequia Races take place. There is a race from St Vincent to Bequia on the Saturday, local races in Admiralty Bay in Bequia on the Sunday, and then the yacht race back to St Vincent on the Monday. We decided to enter Spirit of Cutty Sark and the guys became quite serious about it. All sorts of surplus stuff was offloaded onto Thelma II, a beautiful 70 ft ketch owned by our friend Jeff. By this time Roger's girlfriend Carey had joined us from UK. Along with two additional guys, Clive and Martin, from other yachts anchored in the bay, that made a total of six. Tactics were discussed during our sail over to St Vincent before the start of the race. It was decided to put Clive and Martin on the winches back in the cockpit, leaving Roger and I on deck in readiness to change sails. Carey was in charge of keeping crew watered and fed. We normally only cruised with our main and jib, but for the race out came the large genoa and the spinnaker. The weather was perfect trade-wind sailing, so all sails were put to full use throughout the course, which involved some quick changes. Thanks to Roy's expertise and the sleek design of the boat, Cutty Sark dominated the race from start to finish, and of course we won. We were all exhausted but it was such exhilarating fun. It was quite a contrast to the gentle cruising over the last three months. What a night of celebration we had at the Frangi. During the weekend Bequia was buzzing with spectators and partygoers. As it was a traditional boatbuilding island, the locals took the racing very seriously. Every small boat race throughout Saturday and Sunday was well supported with ear-splitting cheering, and the rum flowed and the music played non-stop. The atmosphere was as good as at any carnival time. What surprised us was how the locals also embraced the yacht race and, knowing who we were, would shout 'Cutty Sark' every time we passed by. With thick heads, and with Jeff from Thelma II joining us as an additional crew member for the return race to St Vincent, we readied ourselves for the start. I remained in the cockpit, leaving Jeff to work the deck with Roger. This time it was a harder race, having to mostly flog to windward involving many tacks. Carey and I spent most of the time sitting on the windward side of the deck to help keep the leeward rails out of the water. Each time the boat tacked we would leap to the other side. It was a far more dramatic race back, but once again we left the fleet behind us and won. Yeh!

The prize-giving was held at the Mariners Inn which was opposite Young Island; a favourite haunt of the yachting fraternity. Not only did we win the BOAC trophy, but we were also presented with all sorts of extras. It included some vibrant, colourful material made from the cotton grown on Mustique – which I was particularly delighted to receive – dinner for two at the Cobblestone Inn, and some champagne, amongst other things. It was one hell of a party that night! The following day, 19 May 1970, some of us went over to Mustique to help celebrate the wedding of Sir John Power and Alison Tracey Cooper – known as Tracey – which was to be held in the newly refurbished Cotton Mill Hotel. Being the end of the season all sorts of people turned up, including Haze from PSV and quite a few of our new friends from St Vincent – Jeff Gunn (one of the twin brothers) and his wife, Lavinia; and Sue and Freddy Harris with Robin Eastwood, who all worked for the Mustique Company which Colin Tenant had formed barely two years previously to start developing the rest of the island. I loved the steel band version of the wedding march. Although most of us didn't know the happy couple, we certainly helped them celebrate it in a very West Indian style. Sadly, I heard later that the marriage only lasted four years. Hey ho!

Chapter 8 – The Rough and the Smooth

Three days later, on the Friday, I flew home. Roy stayed behind to close up the yacht, leaving her safely anchored in Bequia where Jeff from Thelma II would keep an eye on her. By then Roger and Carey were working at the Friendship Bay Hotel. I wanted to leave as soon as possible as I was beginning to suffer from a toe infection, and Roy and I had had a bit of a falling out. Actually, it was a little more than that. When Roy got drunk he was what can only be described as a very happy, loveable soul. The problem was that he would totally forget I was around, and would take off with any available female. When he disappeared it left me angry but also worried. Was he in bed with someone, or had he fallen into a ditch somewhere? Nowadays, putting up with promiscuity is mostly unacceptable, but back then it was not such a big deal to many. This was particularly so in the yachting fraternity. With Roy, it didn't occur often, but each time it did, for me the hurt went deep. It happened at the wedding, and that was just one too many times for me. Roy was as usual very contrite, and tried to persuade me to wait a little longer so we could travel back together, but I had had enough. I was absolutely furious with him but at the same time so very upset. I needed time alone to think seriously about our relationship.

In a sombre mood, I flew LIAT to Barbados and then caught the BOAC flight to Heathrow Airport, then the shuttle bus to Waterloo Station in London. I then limped my way down the taxi rank queue asking if anyone fancied a trip out in the countryside. It wasn't long before someone did, and after agreeing to turn the meter off when it reached £15, we drove to my parents in Ongar. I arrived back on Saturday 23 May. What a surprise for Mum and Dad to see a London taxi turn up on the drive. Dad got so caught up with seeing his long-lost daughter that the poor taxi driver found himself also being welcomed, with lots of handshaking. He happily had a cup of tea with us before heading back to the city.

Whilst I had been away, Mum and Dad had moved into a new council house situated in a small estate at the other end of town. It was a lot bigger and included a garage. I was well impressed, especially for a council house. I thoroughly enjoyed being pampered by Mum over the next few days, and, bless her, she didn't ask any questions about Roy. She could tell something was up and that I wasn't ready to talk about it. She couldn't understand why I wouldn't take up her suggestion to sit in the garden in the sunshine. But I had had enough sunshine and was much happier lounging on the comfortable sofa reading a book. Although most of my clothes were clean, Mum insisted on washing the lot to try and get rid of the smell of boat, whatever that meant.

A trip to the doctors soon sorted out my infected toe, thankfully just in time before Roy turned up on 2 June. My heart did a jump when I saw him unexpectedly drive up in a Lotus Cortina, and I felt so very happy to see him. Having had time to reflect on our relationship, I was still uncertain as to what to do. Was I really prepared to let Roy go? Not wanting to give up my new lifestyle was also clouding the issue. My reaction told me that I still loved him, warts and all. We went for a long walk to talk things through. Roy promised to mend his ways, and assured me he loved me and didn't want us to break up.

Before I knew it we were back to our normal, easy ways with each other. We worked well as a team. The reason why Roy was back in UK was because Leslie needed his help with his new boat. He and Robin Knox-Johnston had joined forces to get enough sponsorship together to purchase an Ocean 71 hull built by Southern Ocean Shipyards – a bigger brother to Spirit of Cutty Sark. They had it transported to Chatham in Kent where a team of mostly volunteers was fitting out the interior in readiness for the two-man Round Britain race due to start on 4 July from Plymouth. They were in an absolute panic to get it ready in time. I was given the job of rushing around getting all sorts of parts, which involved a steep learning curve, mostly regarding plumbing bits. No sooner had I killed one list, another appeared. I tried to help where I could, providing food when it was needed and moving cars around once the boat set off from Chatham. I recall that they only just made the start, and once again those two brilliant sailors proved themselves by winning two days ahead of anyone else.

Whilst that was going on, Roy and I took some time off and looked up May Dale in Lyme Regis. She owned the café down on the Cobb, a small picturesque fishing harbour in Dorset popular with the tourists. We had met her in Bequia where she had a house overlooking Princess Margaret beach in Admiralty Bay. Only a few years previously she had lost her husband Ken, who died one night in his sleep. Poor May woke to find her husband dead by her side. How awful that must have been. The café was frantically busy all the time. Nothing fancy; just good, basic cooking. Working as a waiter in a busy restaurant requires a lot of stamina, so every summer May would employ boys from the local grammar school. She reckoned they were the best. May originally came from Yorkshire and was a larger-than-life lady in her early fifties. She may have been short and dumpy, but the boys knew she would not stand for any nonsense. We stayed in the flat above, enjoying the wonderful view of the harbour and Lyme Bay, and pitched in. Roy was on the till and I helped out in the kitchen preparing the puds. All dead easy stuff that came from catering companies, like banana splits, cassata, and apple pie with cream. Every night it was a race to get the last of the customers out the door so we could get across the road to the pub before closing time. Once in, at closing time the tea towels would go over the pumps and the party began, with May right in the centre of things, often singing her heart out. The local bobby just turned a blind eye. Aching feet and tired bodies were soon forgotten.

We spent some time back in the Gosport area staying with close friends Midge and Graham Young before going to Plymouth to welcome Leslie and Robin back in after their fantastic race. Graham used to be in the navy and was now a salesman for Beckman's Instruments, a company that produced medical equipment. He had an easy-going, laid-back sales approach that was very successful. Midge, on the other hand, was a very active lady who was always busy doing something or other and not afraid to try anything new. Although she was ten years older than me, we became and still are good friends. They had four children ranging from thirteen down to about four – three girls, and the youngest, 'the boy', as Graham would refer to him. I was first introduced to Midge shortly after meeting Roy. When we arrived at her house, she was frantically rushing around trying to tidy up while the two youngest made more mess by creating a tent in the lounge. The reason for the tidying up was that Graham was due back that day. He had been at sea for the past two years. Wow! That was a long time not to see your family, and I don't think servicemen or women are allowed to go for that long nowadays; unless, of course, there is a major crisis.

After leaving Midge and Graham's, we planned to head north via Lyme Regis to offload a pile of stuff at May's. On leaving Gosport, feeling decidedly hungover from a heavy session in The Jolly Roger the night before, Roy suddenly screeched to a halt, reversed back and sat staring at a white Lotus Europa in the front of a small garage. It was for sale.

'I like that,' he said.

'Oh, come on,' I said. 'We've got a long way to go'. One hour later, with stuff poked into every available space, I found myself sitting in the Europa alongside Roy, with the biggest grin ever, speedily heading towards Lyme Regis. I have to say that car was fun to drive. You had to almost lie on your back, and the steering was very direct. I did find it rather skittish in wet conditions, though.

We did an awful lot of driving around the countryside catching up with friends and family, including a rare visit up to Wolverhampton to see Roy's dad and partner Mary. This was the first time I had met them. His dad, Syd, was a larger version of Roy and had that lovely down-to-earth attitude. You could tell immediately that his partner, Mary, had a heart of gold and was the type of person you could depend on getting one huge hug from if you needed it. The reason why they weren't married was that Roy's mother refused to allow a divorce, and by the time the law changed to allow one party to do so, Syd and Mary had been together far too long for it to matter. We stayed for a few days until finally heading back to Ongar to ready ourselves for the return to Bequia and the next season. We left from Heathrow on 25 August 1970 and went via Antigua and St Vincent, finally stepping back on board Cutty Sark two days later. It was unbelievably good being back in Bequia. A little of my heart will always be there. I only have to close my eyes to remember the mixture of smells carried on the soft, warm breeze, and the children, immaculately dressed in their school uniforms, skipping along the dirt track road. It never ceased to amaze me how their mothers managed to keep them so clean, living in such small wooden shacks. It was only in the early sixties that electricity came to the island and a small airstrip was built. And laughter – I shall always remember the happiness of the island's wonderful people.

There was an interesting development on the tip of land at the end of Admiralty Bay, called Moon Hole. A group of houses had been built between the rocks, all positioned so that the rising moon shone through their large Perspex windows. They were owned by escapees from the US, including a couple called Dick and Mary. They had a daughter, Molly. Her parents wanted to set her up in a local business, so with help from a clever designer, the Whaleboner bar was created. What an amazing place. Much of it was made out of whale bones. The bar was made from the backbone and the stools from the vertebrae. Molly was a great party girl and her place became a popular hangout for all us yachties and expats. She had a fantastic body, and I remember seeing a photo of her coming out of the water in Bequia, wearing a very brief bikini, on the front cover of an edition of National Geographic. Another escapee from the States was a chap called Colin, who was very creative. Macramé –a craft of tying knots – was all the rage, and he designed, amongst other things, some very skimpy bikinis which Molly would parade around in. Quite a few of us girls ended up buying them. I did hear that he also designed a very revealing dress for her which she wore at one of Princess Margaret's get-togethers in Mustique. It caused quite a stir amongst her group of men friends; so much so, that apparently Princess Margaret decided to end the party early.

Bequia's history is steeped in boatbuilding and whaling. It

is an amazing sight to witness the capture of a whale. During the months between February and May, humpback whales come down the Bequian channel after having given birth, which sometimes happens on the windward side of the island. A boy is posted on top of the cliff, and when he sees them coming through he blows the conch shell to alert all the families, one of the main families being the Ollivierres who have been whaling for many generations. They use 28 ft wooden sailboats with hand harpoons. First, they go after the calf as that is easy prey. This leaves the mother in a more vulnerable state as she is looking for her lost one. Once the mother is harpooned, the small boats join forces, sailing together to the small island of Petit Nevis (known as Whale Island) and dragging the captured whale behind. By the time they reach the island, the rest of the community are already there and it's like carnival time. The mamas have the big pots in place under fires, ready to melt the blubber, and the rum is flowing. The whale is pulled up the concrete slip and turned over. Once the top layer is removed, men get into the carcass and start cutting off huge chunks of meat which are then passed in a chain up the slope. At the top there are wooden stakes of various heights which determine the proportions of meat allocated to each one. The more a family is involved in the catch, the higher their stake. The whole bay is red with blood, with many sharks feeding off the scraps. All this may sound cruel to many, but one whale keeps a lot of Bequian families in food for most of the year, the oil is used for light and heat, and the bones are made into furniture and other household items. Most of the meat is cooked in its own blubber to last longer. Catching one or two whales a year was their method of survival even in the sixties, and this tradition has continued into the twenty-first century. Whale meat is unique. At first it tastes like beef, but the aftertaste is fishier. It is surprisingly pleasant.

Often we would be among a handful of yachts anchored

in Admiralty Bay, including the island's one and only doctor, Porter Smith, an American from Massachusetts who lived on an old schooner named Christiania along with his hard-working wife and very blonde children. Most mornings we would see them rowing their small wooden dinghy ashore, and, carrying the oars, they would walk up to the local school. Porter and his family would sail around the Grenadines treating the sick. Often the locals couldn't afford to pay him but would do so in kind – a chicken, some fruit or eggs. The private hotel resorts of Mustique, Palm Island and Petit St Vincent supported the family when he came to treat their staff. The old schooner Friendship Rose was the main means of transport between St Vincent and Bequia back then. Apart from passengers, livestock, food, all sorts of hardware and building materials, and even cars were brought across on the boat.

Back to August 1970 ... Poor Cutty Sark had suffered somewhat from being left unused during the summer months. The humidity had really got to her. Every cupboard hinge had seized up, and there was a distinct musky smell below decks. We spent the next few weeks working through all the maintenance items and improvements on the boat. This involved a few trips to St Vincent, which enabled us to catch up with friends including Geoff and Lavinia Gunn. They lived in a lovely house overlooking Young Island. Often we would anchor in the channel there, but we did need to be extra careful when dropping the anchor as the holding ground was not great. I remember on one occasion, whilst having supper with Geoff and Lavinia at their house, they received a phone call from the coastguard alerting us that Cutty Sark was on its way out the channel. It never ceased to amaze me how efficient the jungle drums were out there. We never told anyone where we were going.

During October we ended up doing a yacht delivery to

Miami. It was a lovely old wooden ketch that was in Friendship Bay. The owner decided he wanted to sell her. The boat was stocked up with provisions, and two local men were provided as crew. All Roy and I had to do was step on board and go. We left on 11 October and arrived in St Thomas three days later. Why is it we always seem to arrive at a destination in the small hours of the morning? We couldn't leave St Thomas quick enough. There was rubbish everywhere, and there were far too many dropouts hanging around, high on drugs. That island really was the pits of the Caribbean.

Our two deckhands were brilliant. They were both gentle giants with amazingly polite manners, and they wouldn't allow me to do a thing. They certainly knew how to catch fish and taught me how to make the most amazing fish stew. No expense was spared with the provisions, and we dined mostly on fresh fish and fillet steak. We decided to stop off at Great Inagua in the Bahamas. Wow, what a place! It was full of salt pans going from grey to deep pink with the brine, and we saw so many pink flamingos. It felt as if we were on some alien planet. Unfortunately, it also came with the biggest and juiciest mosquitos. Each of us went ashore armed with a can of Baygon which we were constantly spraying. When you hit one of the buggers, blood splattered right up your arm – yuk! There was just one other boat there. It was in such a dilapidated state we were amazed it was still afloat. It was registered in Haiti and the guys on board were practically in rags. We had so much spare fish on board that we decided to give them some. They were so grateful but insisted in return that we had some of their precious plantain.

We eventually arrived in Miami on 23 October. Knowing the boat agents would be wanting to take details and photos of the boat soon after arriving, the day before I had decided to give below decks a good clean-up, particularly the galley.

As I was cleaning, I saw a cockroach disappear into a small hole in the panelling, so I gave it a hefty spray of Baygon. My screaming brought everyone down below. Hundreds of them came rushing out. Spiders, mice and even snakes do not bother me, but cockroaches I cannot bear. The boys couldn't stop laughing, but I refused to go back down below until they could assure me they had eliminated them. Sure enough, the agents came on board the day after we arrived, so I decided to keep out of the way by going for a walk. We were in a huge marina, but I noticed a park next door so decided to head in that direction. Whilst leaning over an ornamental bridge, watching some carp, I was suddenly aware of a man standing quite close by. I moved away a little, but he sidled right up against me. I then realised there was no one else around. Okay, I thought, don't look at him and don't panic. Just slowly walk away and head back towards the marina. So I did, and he followed. The way back involved walking along a promenade with quite a few seats full of old gentlemen looking out to sea. I thought about heading towards them for safety but figured they wouldn't be able to help much, so I just continued walking. The five minutes' distance seemed like hours, and he was still following at the same pace as mine, keeping just a few feet distance. The boat just had to be at the far end of the marina, didn't it. I got about three quarters of the way across before I panicked and started to run. The chase was on, and he was right behind me. I shot down the finger of pontoons where the boat was at the end, shouting for Roy at the top of my voice. Our two lovely crew were on deck, and to see two huge West Indians coming to my aid sent the guy off in the opposite direction. They wanted to go after him but I stopped them. I just didn't want them getting into any trouble and then have to face the hassle of explanations and reports with the police. That was my only harrowing experience, and to be quite honest I reckon I have been very lucky. You hear of so many other females who haven't been, with far, far worse consequences.

We took a few days off to visit Fort Lauderdale to do some PR work for Cutty Sark, and caught up with some old sailing mates. It was becoming apparent to me that there were a few places around the world where long-distance sailors tended to meet up, normally combined with some sort of regatta. Malta in the Med, Cowes in the Isle of Wight, Antigua, Fort Lauderdale and Newport, Rhode Island, are the main ones. It's certainly weird when you meet up with someone you haven't seen for say two or three years – you just pick up the conversation where it left off, normally over copious amounts of beer. No one shows any real big surprises at meeting – it is all rather taken for granted that you will meet up again somewhere, sometime. Often boxes of reading books get swapped and sailing updates are noted.

We eventually returned to Bequia on 5 November, this time via Grenada, only to find that Roger and Carey had got married in Mustique whilst we were away. We were so disappointed to have missed the occasion. The date had been fixed before they realised we were not going to be around. As Roger and Carey had decided to continue working at Friendship Bay Hotel, our new crew member was going to be my sister's boyfriend, Richard. He was a car mechanic by trade, and although he had no sailing experience, he was a hard worker and quick to learn. This pleased Roy as he was able to teach Richard from scratch to do things in proper naval fashion. He flew out to join us on the eighteenth, just a few days before our first charter of the season. We were then working flat out. Not only did we have quite a few weekly bookings, but we also filled in some of the gaps with daily trips out of Young Island.

We managed to get to PSV for the Christmas Day party, but unfortunately, thanks to our charterers it was somewhat spoilt.

I had prepared all sorts of traditional Christmas fare, carefully avoiding pork as I knew the family were Jewish. What I didn't realise was that they were VERY Jewish and flatly refused to show any recognition that Christmas existed, even for us. We were on a dream yacht anchored in one of the most beautiful, exclusive islands in the Grenadines, surrounded by crystal clear turquoise water in perfect weather conditions, and what was I doing? Sobbing my heart out, sitting on the coach roof. I was homesick and missed England's cold weather. Crazy. Fortunately, it didn't last long, and by the evening I was dancing with the best to a steel band, fairly loaded with rum punches, saying to hell with our grumpy charterers. I think they were the worst bunch we had to look after. Most families or groups were great fun and gave embarrassingly good feedback.

On 8 January 1971, the French cruise ship SS Antilles went aground off Mustique. It just so happened we were back in Bequia. The captain had decided to take the ship close in to the island through a wide channel whilst the passengers were enjoying pre-dinner drinks and watching the sunset. What he didn't realise was that there was a large uncharted rock in the middle of this channel which was well known by the locals and us yachties. The force of hitting the rock burst one of the ship's fuel lines. In no time at all the ship was engulfed in fire and the cry to abandon ship was raised. As soon as we heard the SOS, those of us anchored in Bequia rushed to their assistance. Being a lot lighter and faster than the rest of the fleet, we sailed rather than motored across to Mustique. A few of the life rafts managed to safely reach the island's beach. By then the Queen Elizabeth II cruise ship had reached the scene, and they picked up a large proportion of the passengers and crew, and headed to Barbados. Some of the yachts picked up a few survivors, mainly crew members. We decided to drift with the tide for a final check and came across a life raft that had been missed.

It contained the captain and the last of the crew to leave the ship. The poor captain sat on top of the cabin on Cutty Sark in a daze, repeatedly saying, 'The rock was not charted,' in broken English. Whilst sailing back to Bequia I managed to clean some of the oil from the men's faces and hands, and gave them hot drinks. We finally arrived back around midnight. One of the other yachts had picked up the purser, who had the list of passengers and crew. Unfortunately, due to the captain of the Queen Elizabeth II giving strict instructions for the tannoy system not to be used for the rest of the night, checking that all passengers and crew were safe was delayed for some hours. Consequently, some vessels continued searching the stricken area for longer than was necessary. Remarkably, no one was lost. The SS Antilles finally broke in two, making a sad scene for sightseeing.

The wreck of SS Antilles did attract more interest from guests on Young Island, so we started to do day trips to Mustique which worked out to be quite lucrative. This was perfect timing as our next charter booking was not due to start until the end of the month. We ended up doing two or three trips each week, which left plenty of time to relax. It made a lovely break not having any guests living on board, and I certainly didn't miss the rushing around between charters. We happily remained anchored off Young Island, enjoying plenty of socialising with our St Vincent chums. What an idyllic time we were having, and once again I found myself reflecting on what a very lucky girl I was. On the morning of 25 January we picked up six guests from Young Island who had booked us for a day trip to Mustique. We had been up quite late the night before, propping up the bar at the Mariners Inn, so once everyone had been served some drinks and was comfortably sitting in the cockpit, I signalled to Roy that I was going below for a kip. I must have been tired as I went into a deep sleep, and woke with a start to hear Roy calling that we were coming into Mustique and they needed my assistance. Still feeling groggy, I rushed up on deck to give a hand. If only I had not had that sleep.

Chapter 9 – A Traumatic Time

Mustique had a wooden jetty, and due to the usual swell in the bay we tended to tie up stern-to to the jetty to allow the guests to stretch their legs ashore and do a little exploring whilst I prepared lunch for them. I came up on board and grabbed the extra-long line needed from the locker, tied a bowline in one end and threw it down on the stern deck. By then Richard had dropped the sails, and Roy was motoring close to the jetty for me to lasso one of the two bollards. Once done, I started to let the line out whilst the yacht headed out at right angles for Richard to drop the anchor. Unfortunately, in my haste I had grabbed the bottom end of the coil, causing the line to jump out of the coil and tangle. As we were going quite slowly, I sat down and unravelled each loop of the line as the slack was taken up. One of the loops caught round my right ankle and, before I realised, it was pulling me towards the stern cleat that the line was running through. I yelled for Roy to stop. Although he quickly threw the engine into full astern, it was too late. As the boat slowly corrected itself from going forward to backwards, I sat there watching my foot twist right round and then pull away from my leg. I could do nothing except watch and scream. It all seemed to happen in very slow motion. There was no real pain – just a very hot feeling.

I suppose I was lucky as it could have been worse. Feeding the line through the cleat meant that my foot took the full force by jamming the line at this point. By the time the hefty cleat sprang from its fittings the boat had corrected itself, giving enough slack to release me from the rope. It stopped me going overboard with the risk of drowning. There were two other yachts anchored in the bay, and what unbelievable luck: on one was a fully trained nurse looking after the owner's wife. Within a few minutes of her hearing my screams I was injected with morphine. On the other yacht, not only was one of the guests a doctor but an orthopaedic surgeon from the States. He took one look at the damage and told Roy to feed my foot to the fishes as there was no hope of saving it. The line we used was an old halyard, and being pre-stretched Terylene it cut through my ankle like a cheese cutter, sealing everything as it went. I therefore lost very little blood and had third-degree burns round the area.

My luck continued. At that time Mustique was one of the few smaller islands that had an airstrip, and a two-seater airplane had just landed to deliver some mail and produce. The passenger seat was taken out, and Frankie the nurse and I were squeezed in. Before leaving the boat, being quite high on morphine, apparently I gave Roy very explicit instructions on what to serve up for lunch to our six guests on board. I was also full of apologies for spoiling their day. Needless to say, at that stage no one was hungry. Within an hour I was in the little operating room at St Vincent hospital. That flight saved me having to endure a good four hours of uncomfortable windward sailing. I found out afterwards that Frankie, with one glance at the operating room, took charge of washing down and mopping up. The jungle drums were beating fast. By the time I was ready to be operated on, a spare set of tools had arrived from a US surgeon who was doing some voluntary work in St

Lucia. How they got there so quickly I shall never know. After the operation, once Frankie knew I was going to be okay she rejoined her yacht before I was able to thank her. I didn't even have her full name and contact details. This really upset me.

I had a truly remarkable experience in St Vincent hospital. The staff were amazing. Dr Gun-Munroe, (who later became Sir Gun-Munroe, Governor General of St Vincent and the Grenadines) performed the operation. All he did was save as much as possible and seal the wound to avoid gangrene setting in. I was kept in a very comfortable and happy state due to being well dosed with penicillin and morphine. When I started to dream of the needle going in a few days later, I insisted the morphine was stopped. I was thoroughly spoilt whilst in that hospital. The nurses insisted that I held every baby that was born whilst I was there. They would bring each tiny black baby to me once it had been washed and weighed. I got the first cuddle before its mother! On every occasion the nurse would say, 'It's the way of de Lord.' Every single person who came to visit someone in the hospital would also come to see me, including the taxi drivers. Apparently, a board and easel were put up at the entrance to indicate the way to my room!

Cath and Martin from the Cobblestone Inn insisted that they provided me with lunch and supper every day during my stay in hospital. I cannot thank them enough for their generosity. When in St Vincent, we used the Black Cat Laundry, and the very next day after I arrived in hospital they sent a boy along to collect my dirty nightie, returning it clean the following day, beautifully wrapped with a ribbon. This they did every day throughout my stay in hospital. How did they find out about my accident so quickly? One thing that really delighted me was when one of the skippers set up a spare ship-to-shore radio in my room. This meant that I could keep in touch not only with Roy but also the rest of the charter fleet, bringing me up to date with their movements and gossip. The nurses were fascinated with what was to them new technology. They would pop in when they had a spare moment and giggle away when they heard a voice. Fortunately, one of the yachts was laid up and Roy was able to borrow their cook/hostess for the rest of the charter season, so we didn't lose any of our bookings. I had so many visitors I didn't exactly get a lot of rest during the day, but that didn't seem to bother me. I was in no pain and slept well at night.

Roy had his birthday two days after the accident, and friends organised a surprise birthday tea in my room complete with an enormous chocolate cake with one big fat candle in the middle of it. One of my visitors was Mrs Barnard (second or third generation English) whom I barely knew. She very kindly came with a bunch of roses that she had picked from her own garden. This would have been quite a generous gift as I believe roses don't grow easily in the salty West Indian climate. I was also visited by all the guests who were on board the boat at the time of the accident. They came loaded with beautiful gifts including some very pretty baby-doll pyjamas. I could see the sadness in their eyes and tried to reassure them that I would be okay. I was fit and strong, and at twenty-two I had youth on my side. I wasn't about to let losing a foot ruin my life and knew even then I would bounce back. It was such a pity their holiday was marred by the accident.

Roy had alerted Les, and he in turn contacted the insurance company. They immediately flew out someone from Lloyds of London. Sue, Freddie and Robin were on a mission. They were determined for me to get maximum compensation. The poor chap didn't know what hit him. In the process of making sure he was being well entertained Robin discovered he was gay, which abruptly stopped her in her tracks. We were all in hysterics. He did come and visit me, and gave me a pretty mirror and comb set as a gift, so I reckon my chums did a good job. Soon after I was admitted to hospital Julie from Young Island sent over their carpenter to measure me for crutches. Just before I left hospital, he returned with the most beautifully made and varnished set. I had yet another moment of feeling totally overwhelmed.

On the day of my discharge from hospital, 11 February, Roy went to pay the bill only to discover someone had already done so. To this day I don't know who it was and can only thank that person from afar. Before being taken over to Freddie and Susie's, we stopped off at the Cobblestone Inn so that I could say a big thank you to Cath and Martin for keeping me so well fed during my stay in hospital. Whilst having a cold drink there Colin Tennant, with a group of people came in, looking very much the eccentric English gentleman that he was. He was wearing one of his pyjama-type suits, a large-brimmed hat and, as usual, carrying his cane. As soon as he spotted me, he came over to offer his condolences and then asked if we wanted the rope back.

'No thank you,' said I.

'Oh good,' said Colin. 'I want to put it in the little museum we have.' I looked at the stunned faces around me and burst out laughing. It was just the sort of thing you would expect to hear from Colin.

Once we arrived at the Harris's house, Susie busied herself preparing lunch whilst we relaxed with some cold drinks. After eating her delicious food, I don't know who came up with the idea but we ended up playing a fun game of croquet. There was a lot of laughter with Susie running after me with a chair for me to sit on so I could swing the mallet. I well and truly christened my beautiful crutches that afternoon.

So here I was, sipping my lime squash, once again admiring the view. Where to from here? I wondered. Am I worried about the future? Absolutely not! I am still on an adventure, and losing a foot isn't going to put a stop to that. Okay, I know I will need to get back to England to sort myself out first, but that will be just a little setback.

I was determined not to give up my current lifestyle. I think I must have been left alone for quite some time but all of a sudden I was aware of everyone coming towards me, with Freddy holding the phone. He handed it to me and I could hear a ringing tone.

'It's ringing your home,' said Freddy.

I had no time to prepare for this, and all of a sudden I could hear Mum's voice saying, 'Hello?'

I gulped. 'Hello, Mum. Now don't get upset – I'm okay, but I've had an accident. I've lost my foot.'

I didn't have a chance to say anything else as Mum immediately broke down and started to cry hysterically. I could hear Dad in the background asking what the matter was. Between sobs, she managed to tell him I had lost my foot. Dad's answer was, 'Is that all?' The poor love was by then expecting to hear the absolute worse. It did stop Mum crying, and whilst she was berating Dad, he grabbed the phone from her.

'Hello, love – now what do you want me to do?' Good ol' Dad went straight into practical mode. He was going to discuss the matter with our family doctor and find out who was the best orthopaedic surgeon operating out of our local hospital. Once he knew the date of my return, he would then make an appointment for me to see him as soon as possible. I assured Dad I was okay and being well looked after at this end, and told him to give Mum a big hug and tell her not to get too upset; it was only a silly old foot!

I managed to hold it together during the call but once I ended it, I broke down and really sobbed. Hearing Mum and Dad's voices shattered the brave front I had kept up till then.

It had to be the worse phone call ever. I had been dreading making it for some days and kept putting it off until I was left with no option when Freddy thrust the phone in my hand. I was an emotional wreck, and it took me a while to pull myself together. Loads of hugs and tissues later, and a stiff rum drink, my smile was back in place but boy, was I exhausted.

After spending the day with Freddie and Susie I was taken to Young Island, where it had been arranged for Julie and Simon to take care of me until I flew back to England the following week.

I was extremely well looked after. Julie and Simon could not have done more for me. The following day Roy took me for a sail over to Bequia. He wanted to make sure that I wouldn't develop a phobia of sailing. As if I would. He was feeling very guilty about the accident and blamed himself heavily. We talked through all the details of the accident over and over again, which helped us both. I reckon getting something like that out in the open is the best thing you can do, and it puts a stop to any hang-ups. It certainly was not Roy's fault – only my own stupidity. First, handling the rope wrongly, and then not getting Roy to stop the boat when the rope first started to get tangled up. It was good to have that quiet time together before I left to return to the UK.

We planned my flight home to coincide with an American couple, Roger and Peg, who were leaving Young Island to spend a few days in their villa in Barbados before heading back to New York. Roger was fantastic. In no uncertain terms, and in a way that only a successful American business man can do, he made sure BOAC were well aware they would be flying back an invalid who needed lots of care That night I stayed with Roger and Peg, and the following afternoon a taxi took all three of us to the airport. When we arrived, a nurse with a wheelchair was waiting for me. I only just managed to give Roger and

Peg a big thank-you hug before I was whisked off. Customs and Immigration was a blur, and before I knew it, I was seated in the Super VC10 plane ready for take-off. They made up a bed for me on the three front seats just before the first-class section. It was champers and first-class food all the way home, and just before landing they carried me into the cockpit. Whilst having breakfast with the crew, I sat listening to the BBC news on headphones, flying over the white cliffs of Dover. I can't see that happening nowadays, even in my invalid state. On arrival at Heathrow I was bustled off the plane by a rather large bossy Irish nurse, once again customs and immigration being virtually ignored. It would have been a brave person to have waylaid her and her charge.

I arrived back in England on 19 February. It was lovely seeing Mum and Dad waiting for me. What an emotional time. It didn't take long to drive home, where my two sisters were waiting to see me. Janet was now twenty, and my kid sister, Karen, nine. After lots of cuddles and tears we began to discuss the way forward. We are a very practically minded family. Once they received my telegram notifying them of my flight details, Dad got our family doctor to arrange an appointment with Mr Fisk, an orthopaedic surgeon who came highly recommended. He normally operated out of one of the London hospitals but did do some work from our local hospital in Harlow. I was to see him in just a few days' time. As it turned out, I saw his assistant, who explained I had two options. They could either make good where the break was above the ankle or perform an amputation six inches below the knee. If I went for the first option then I would end up with a rather clumpy artificial foot that wouldn't look good cosmetically and, due to being at the thin part of the leg, would give limited support and mean that I would always have a limp. The second option would enable a better-fitting prosthesis, well supported and with little or no limp. To me it was a no-brainer, and although he recommended I think about it, I assured him my decision was to amputate. I just wanted to start walking again as soon as possible. This was when the blow came. The NHS waiting list was four to six months. No way did I want to wait that long. When I asked how long it would be as a private patient, the answer was I could have the operation the following week. The cost would be roughly £1,600, which in 1971 was an awful lot of money. This also meant that Mr Fisk himself would perform the operation. With little hesitation and after taking a deep breath, I said to go ahead, and a date was set for the following week. At that point I had no idea how I was going to pay for it. Thankfully, no deposit was required.

That night I sat down with Mum and Dad to discuss how I was going to pay for the operation. I knew that eventually the insurance company would cover the costs, but it could take some time before a settlement was agreed. In the meantime, I needed a loan. I knew Roy or my mum and dad didn't have that sort of money, and borrowing from the bank didn't come into the equation. I don't know why, because looking back they probably would have agreed. It was just not done so readily back then. My dad's mum, Granny, was the only one in the family who had that kind of spare money, but I wasn't sure I should ask as she was eighty-six. Would it be too much of a worry for her, and what would the rest of the family think?

My gran was quite a character. She lost her husband in the First World War in the French trenches. This left her to bring up four kids, my dad being the baby, without any support. Her mother came from a wealthy family but ran away to marry a tradesman. She was therefore disinherited. On her father's deathbed his heart softened. His solicitor tried to trace her but didn't succeed in time. Her husband also had no family. This situation forced my gran into service. She worked hard to keep her children clothed and fed, and Dad was mostly brought up by his sister, Cissie, and his older brothers, George and Richard. At the grand age of seventy she met and married a seventy-five-year-old gentleman who was a provincial Grand Master of the Freemasons and lived in a big old Victorian house round the corner from where she lived in Thorpe Bay, near Southend. When he died six years later, she promptly went to Paris to enjoy the sights and shows. Although he left most of his money to a local boys' school, Gran did have enough to comfortably live on with some to spare.

Gran was more than happy to loan me the money, especially after I promised to pay her back with interest within two years A few days later I was admitted into Princess Alexandra Hospital in Harlow. Boy, what a difference to St Vincent. The staff made it quite clear that they did not approve of private patients. My room was opposite the area used to empty bed pans. Consequently, I had very little sleep. When I came to after the operation, it felt like my leg was on fire. On investigation it was discovered Elastoplast had been used, even after I told them I was allergic to it. As I had just come out of a general anaesthetic, they couldn't give me any more drugs. Instead they poured a glass of sherry down my throat before two nurses firmly held me down whilst another pulled off the dressing. Unbelievable! A great deal of fuss was made because I was entitled to choose from a special menu. I remember one day I had steak and it was decidedly off. It was actually green. A lot of tutting was made when I refused to eat it. I also suffered from bed sores due to the amount of starch used on the bed linen. The only good thing was Mr Fisk and his team. The operation was a success, and I ended up with a good shape stump, which apparently makes all the difference to having a comfortable and well-fitting prosthesis. After six days Mr Fisk came to see me, and I asked when I could be discharged. His reply was that I would have to get used to using crutches before I could leave. I was determined not to stay in that hospital a minute longer than necessary, and immediately demonstrated my ability to not only walk the length of the corridor but also to go up and down the stairs. With great relief I was discharged later that day.

Once I got home, life became somewhat boring and frustrating. I only had to blink and my wonderful attentive mother would be at hand wanting to assist. I loved my family dearly, but I needed space and my independence back. Old school friends came to visit me with huge bunches of flowers and very embarrassed faces. You see, with my surname being Pegg I was sometimes called Pegg Leg at school. We had a good laugh about it; strange how things turn out.

I decided to head down to Gosport on the Hampshire coast. This was close to my last posting in the Wrens and where a lot of my sailing friends lived, including Roger and Carey who had returned from Bequia due to Carey being pregnant. I also needed to get some sort of car. Roy had already been in touch with a car dealer friend down there to sort me out. It was decided that my sister Janet and I would go down to pick up a car which she would then bring back to Essex, leaving me to stay awhile with my friends. As Dad was foreman on a building site in East London, he offered to drop us off at Waterloo Station rather than use the underground train service from Ongar. Dad left us at the main entrance, and it wasn't until he shot off that we saw a vast number of steps that had to be climbed.

'No problem,' said I. 'You bump up the wheelchair, and I will slowly hop up all the stairs with the aid of one crutch and the stair rail.'

This was happening during the rush hour. After some difficulty, Janet got the heavy wheelchair that we had borrowed from the NHS to the top and turned it to face down the stairs, ready for me to climb into. Before we realised what had happened, a young chap grabbed hold of the chair and ran it down the stairs, thinking he was being very helpful, and then carried on rushing off to work. We looked at each other and howled with laughter. We ended up sitting on the grubby stairs, tears rolling down our faces, amidst masses of rushing commuters who must have thought we were either mad or high as coots on drugs.

Two weeks with Roger and Carey made all the difference. They lived just down from The Jolly Roger in Hardway, which is part of Gosport. Their house was one of a row of detached Victorian cottages, and was a wedding present from Roger's dad. What made it amazing was the view from their large lounge window which was at the back of the property on the second level. It overlooked the top end of Portsmouth harbour. It was so lovely to see water again and I never got tired of that view. There was always a lot of boating activity, and anchored in the centre of this wide expanse of water was the beautiful three-masted frigate TS Foudroyant that had been built in 1812. She was being used as a cadet training ship. Now you will find her in a royal naval museum in Hartlepool under her original name of HMS Trincomalee.

I returned home a lot happier and the family became more relaxed around me. I now had to be patient and wait until all the swelling on my stump went down before I could be fitted with an artificial leg. In the meantime, I had to bandage up my stump as tightly as possible to help maintain a good even shape. During this time there was a family get-together at my aunt and uncle's over in Worcester Park, South-West London. Uncle Tom was a bit of a comedian to say the least. They met on stage whilst serving in the Royal Air Force during the war. Aunty Sylvia was a can-can girl and Uncle Tom was larking about with famous comedians the Marx Brothers. Since the war, Uncle still played the comedian on stage with an amateur local group, whilst Aunty was kept busy making the various costumes. Often the Chelsea Pensioners were entertained by the group. Whilst Mum and Aunty were catching up before lunch, Dad, Uncle Tom, my two cousins Keith and Kevin, and my sister Janet and I disappeared down to the local pub. We ended up having quite a session with a few of Uncle's mates. Pushing the wheelchair back in a straight line was definitely a challenge for my dear Uncle Tom and caused a great deal of giggling. Once we reached home, our beaming faces fell a little when we saw Mum and Aunty. We were rather late for lunch. I pushed myself out of the wheelchair, saying 'Shhorrry,' and promptly fell over. I had completely forgotten I was minus a foot. My stump hit the tiled hallway quite hard, which split open the carefully stitched end. It was only a little bit and didn't really hurt too much thanks to the number of gin and tonics I had drunk. At least it stopped the telling off we were about to get, as everyone went into concern mode. 'You owe me one for that,' I whispered to Uncle Tom, knowing he would have got the brunt of it.

Chapter 10 – Don't Stop Me Now

It was now April, and the end of the charter season. At long last Roy was on his way back with Spirit of Cutty Sark. Leslie wanted to give the charter scene in the Med a go. It was about this time that I heard about two other nasty incidents that had happened in the Grenadines within a month of my accident. They say trouble comes in threes. First, a girl working on a lovely old traditional 90 ft ketch lost all her fingertips on one hand whilst trying to close a heavy wooden hatch. The second incident was a lot closer to home. Our good friend Jeff was sailing back to St Vincent, having dropped off some charterers in Grenada. His yacht Thelma II, an old 70 ft wooden ketch, sprung a plank close to the bottom of the keel. Unfortunately, he wasn't able to do any temporary repairs as a water tank had been added above it, and the bilge pump couldn't keep up with the intake of water. As the bow was getting lower and lower, Jeff decided it was time to abandon ship. When they discovered the life raft was perished, he put two of the crew, a girl and a guy, into the dory (fibreglass tender to the yacht but without the outboard motor) whilst Jeff and the remaining crew member grabbed the mini sail minus its sail. A mini sail is rather like a surfboard with a small sail. Just before leaving the yacht Jeff managed to put out an SOS giving his estimated position, but due to the boat getting heavier and slower with the intake of water, his estimated position was incorrect. The search at first light therefore was concentrated in an area a lot further north from Grenada. The two in the dory were thankfully found within twenty-four hours. Jeff and the other member of the crew were eventually picked up three days later. Although they were both extremely dehydrated and had lost a layer of skin on their backs, they were still alive. Jeff recovered physically, but not so well mentally. He went from drinking a couple of beers a day to consuming a great deal of hard liquor by the bottle. He also suffered financially as all his money was tied up in the yacht and I believe he was not adequately insured. A few years later he was arrested attempting to smuggle a ton of hash into Florida, and ended up spending some time in an open state prison in Pensacola. He was then deported and sent back to Canada, where I believe he became a tug driver.

I eventually got the long-awaited ship-to-shore phone call from Roy saying he was just off the coast of Cornwall. My sister Janet was also waiting for news as her boyfriend was our crew member Richard. We headed down to the River Hamble with Janet driving my car, followed by a couple of her friends in theirs in order to bring Janet and Richard back to Essex. It took Roy three days to work their way up to the Hampshire coast due to lack of wind and diesel. Their trip back from the West Indies was horrendous with them battling with one depression after the other. They were all so exhausted. Whilst waiting for them to arrive I stayed with Sue and Robin Knox-Johnston. In 1969 Robin gained fame by being the first person to sail singlehanded and non-stop around the world, in a 32 ft wooden ketch named Suhaili, for which he was awarded a CBE and later knighted. There was great relief all round when Cutty Sark was finally sighted entering Southampton Water. After a couple of days resting up, we came back to my folks' house to gather ourselves together and decide what to do next. The workforce were already stripping out Cutty Sark and getting her ready to take to the Med. At some stage later Chay Blyth, known for his singlehanded non-stop voyage round the world going westward, acquired Cutty Sark and lent it to Naomi James for her 1977 singlehanded round the world voyage – the first woman to achieve this. By then it had been altered into a ketch rig and renamed Express Crusader.

Within a few days of our return to Ongar, I received a phone call from Gerald, a local farmer. He had heard of my accident from an article written about me in the local newspaper. He was originally from New Zealand and was a pilot in the Second World War. He had lost his leg whilst motor racing in France quite a few years previously. Gerald had bought a 40 ft catamaran which was just being completed in a boatyard in Brightlingsea on the Essex coast. He wanted Roy and me to take it round to 'somewhere nice' in the Med. He wouldn't take no for an answer and said we were to take our time. He felt it was important for me to get back to sailing as soon as possible, and this was an ideal opportunity for him to have the boat based in warmer waters where he and his family could enjoy more favourable sailing. He also insisted that I borrowed a car of his for as long as I wished. It was a Mini but had no clutch. It wasn't an automatic but instead had pre-selected gears. This meant I could drive it with just one foot. I really enjoyed driving that car round the Essex lanes, and gaining that little bit of independence made me feel more normal. Gerald also owned a six-seater twin engine Cessna aeroplane. As much of Essex is very flat, several airfields were built there during the war. Gerald's farm included one of the old runways, which he made full use of.

Over the next few weeks, whilst waiting for Gerald's boat to be completed, I had regular physio sessions at the Douglas

Bader Unit, which is part of the Roehampton Limb Fitting Centre in London, in order to get my right leg muscles working again. Douglas Bader was the pilot who, after losing both legs in a flying accident, with sheer dogged determination managed to convince the RAF that he was still capable of flying with the aid of his two prostheses. During the Battle of Britain his squadron of Spitfires brought down sixty-seven German aircraft. He was and still is a great inspiration to all limbless people, including myself. Whilst up at Roehampton I also made use of the physio pool. To my great surprise, when I started to swim I kept rolling over. My body was not used to the imbalance of weight, and it took three sessions before my brain and body made the adjustment. From then on I was back to swimming well again, although not as strong as before due to only having one foot to propel me. It was a good job I was left-handed so that I could make use of my stronger arm to stop me swimming round in circles. Gone were the days of being able to use flippers.

The first appointment with my limb fitter was coming up, so we decided that we would set sail soon afterwards. I would go back to Roehampton a few weeks later to pick up my new leg and then return to wherever we had left the boat. Both doctor and limb fitter agreed that this was a good idea, especially psychologically. I would be concentrating on keeping both legs steady on a moving deck, which would hopefully prevent me from developing any unnecessary limp. Also, a catamaran was a lot steadier than a monohull, which meant there would be less rolling and no heeling over when sailing close to the wind. So, after having a plaster cast of my stump made, Roy and I set off from Brightlingsea. It was by now late June, a lovely time of the year to go. We decided not to take any crew with us – just three legs between us. Night shifts were done two hours on and two hours off. We felt that doing more than two hours alone would run the risk of falling asleep. I was quite surprised how quickly our bodies adjusted to short bursts of sleep. During the day we would extend the timing of the shifts to allow each of us to catch up by grabbing a few extra hours of kip.

We had wonderful sailing weather, averaging around eight knots – a graceful and easy pace for a fast catamaran. Even the Bay of Biscay was calmer than normal, making for very pleasant sailing on a broad reach. Perfect conditions like that make you realise how lucky you are to be doing what many others only dream of. Out at sea, away from most of the land's pollution, everything seems a lot clearer, and when the weather is kind, it's so wonderfully peaceful. On a cloudless night you see a lot more stars, with the moon giving off plenty of light, even when it's just a small slither. Without man-made light, your eyes adjust to see so much more. I love watching the effervescence off the water as the boat slices through the waves – it's so mesmerising, sending me into a dreamlike state, at peace with myself and the world. Nothing I know of can compare with such a calming experience. You are alone, a very tiny spec bobbing up and down in a vast area of water – a truly awesome feeling, especially when you are well out to sea, out of sight of land, lights and any signs of habitation. When you are far away from pollution, dawn and dusk can be breathtakingly spectacular. Every shade of red and orange is thrown across the sky in amazing sweeps of colour, creating fanciful patterns with any clouds that get in their way. Even in my early twenties, when I took so much for granted, some of the more memorable sunsets and sunrises succeeded in stirring up tearful emotions. I have seen many a tough guy being affected by such heavenly beauty.

It was whilst in the Bay of Biscay, on one of my two-hour night shifts, that I came across an escaped fisherman's buoy drifting with a large amount of seaweed. From a distance it took on the appearance of a floating body. When Roy came up to relieve me I told him about this, laughing it off and blaming the calm conditions for making me too fanciful. It did make me think, though. What would you do if you did come across a dead body? What if you were too far offshore to use the radio? Do you just leave it and head for the nearest coast, which may be a distance away, or would you try to bring the body onboard? That could be quite gruesome, especially if your SOS was not picked up for some time. Such horrible thoughts, and I just hoped it would never happen.

In no time at all we rounded Cape Finistere and headed down the north Spanish coast. We decided to stop off in Vigo to restock on fresh supplies and water. Having just the one leg, I used my bottom a lot, and thanks to having plenty of grab rails around the boat, it was easy to hop around the deck. Due to having played quite a lot of squash whilst in the navy and the amount of deck work done more recently, I had strong arms, and these were now beginning to get even stronger. So, I was able to down the sails, get the fenders and mooring ropes ready, and have the deck looking neat and tidy before coming alongside the fuel dock. Often when entering a town dock, quite a few spectators would be watching. Amongst them inevitably would be some retired fishermen sucking on their pipes, critically watching how yachtsmen handled their vessels, often being well entertained when things didn't quite go to plan. Vigo was no exception, but this time they did more than just sit and be entertained. As soon as they realised I was attempting to moor the boat with just one leg and with no other help, four well-seasoned old guys sprang up, two of them jumping on board like spring lambs, taking the rope from my hand, and with much waving of arms and shouting in Spanish, in no time at all the boat was safely tied up. Roy and I both thanked them with what little Spanish we knew, and after lots of handshaking, the odd hug and thumbs up, they returned to their bench and the business of relighting their pipes. I was left to supervise the refuelling of our water and diesel tanks, whilst Roy went off armed with a list to find the nearest bank and supermarket.

The weather remained good all the way to the Straits of Gibraltar and into the Mediterranean. We decided to make the most of the weather and not stop at Gibraltar but continue on until we reached one of the new marinas that were springing up along the Spanish coast. We wanted to get as far up the coast as possible before the mistral arrived, a strong wind that develops in the Med in late summer. When it's in full force it's virtually impossible for small boats, and sometimes even the fishing fleet, to get through the Straits of Gibraltar. We were sailing from headland to headland and, now in the middle of the summer season, the beaches were just a mass of pink bodies. We were beginning to look like a seaside shop as we kept picking up small inflatable play rafts, lilos and balls. We had just passed Alicante when Roy called me. I was having an afternoon nap down below.

'Come up, Terri, and prepare yourself for a bit of a shock,' he said.

I sprung up wondering what on earth the matter was. Still rubbing sleep from my eyes, following Roy's pointed finger, I was stunned to see a dead body just off our port side. It was so unbelievable, especially after having such recent thoughts of this possibility happening. Thank goodness we were not far from shore. It was quite badly bloated and very smelly. Fortunately, the body was face down. We manoeuvred the boat so that we had it between the two hulls. I was then able to lean down on the trampoline and get quite close to the body. It was a man dressed in jeans and deck shoes with no top on, with layers of skin peeling off his back. I was looking for any item or markings – a watch, ring, tattoos –that would help identify the man. Sadly, there was nothing. Whilst I was doing this, Roy flashed an SOS with our Aldis lamp to a fishing boat that was a little way off. When they eventually came over, we pointed to the body and indicated quite clearly that they should use one of their nets to pick it up. All they did was shrug their shoulders, with one of them pinching his nose, and then took off. We couldn't believe they were so callous. If we had tried to get the body on board ourselves, it would have just broken up. Apart from knowing someone, somewhere, would be looking for this poor soul, once the tide turned it would take the body into the bay and towards the beach. Once it hit the surf it would start to fall apart. I had visions of young children coming across bits of body. Imagine a young child finding the head. It didn't bear thinking about.

Once Roy carefully charted where the body was, we turned around and headed back into Alicante. We decided the best thing to do was to drop anchor and go over to the yacht club by dinghy. Not only did we reckon the body could well be a yachtsman because of the deck shoes worn, but hopefully we would find someone there able to speak English. A lot of the better-known Spanish yacht clubs tend to be rather exclusive, and Alicante was certainly one of them. At that time, apart from the one in Tenerife, access to these clubs was strictly members only. When we got to their jetty, not only was there a large notice in English confirming this, there was also a man employed to make sure this was obeyed. He caught up with us once we had climbed out of the dinghy, and was standing on the jetty. Whilst I was standing there on crutches, Roy tried patiently to explain it was imperative we spoke to someone who understood English, about something important. The man would not or could not understand our request, and pushed Roy and then me, albeit gently, back towards our dinghy with a torrent of Spanish. Roy is an extremely amiable guy and rarely loses his temper, but this was one of the times he did.

Pushing the man to one side, telling him to get out of his way, he stomped off down the jetty telling me to follow. The genteel peace of the marble-clad reception hall of the yacht club was soon shattered as first Roy barged in wearing a rather tatty pair of shorts, faded T-shirt and flip-flops, followed by me similarly dressed on crutches, and an angry employee waving his arms in true Latin fashion whilst firing off rapid bursts of Spanish.

Fortunately, there was a lady member present who calmly spoke to the employee who promptly disappeared, muttering furiously. She then sat us down and asked in perfect English how she could help. As soon as she grasped the situation, tea was ordered for us whilst she headed off to the phone. A little while later she returned to let us know that a police launch was already on its way out into the bay to pick up the body. She then explained that a couple of weeks ago, three of their members went out in a yacht and never returned. Although searches had been going on for some time, not one of the men or the yacht had been found. As no distress call was made, it was a complete mystery as to what had happened. She felt fairly certain that this was one of their missing members. Quite surprisingly, the police didn't require a statement from us and were happy for us to continue with our journey. After many thanks from more than one member we returned to our boat, and after spending the night in the bay, continued our journey the following morning. We often wondered afterwards what really happened. Drug smuggling was quite active then. This we knew through Jeff. He had started his disastrous trip from England, where he bought the yacht, and was instructed to be off Algiers by a certain time on a certain date. The ton of hash was then delivered to him by a fast motor launch. We had heard stories of an occasional yacht being hijacked, the crew killed and thrown overboard, enabling the boat to be used to smuggle drugs. It would then be scuttled out at sea, destroying all evidence. Algiers was not that far away.

It wasn't long before we were sailing along the French Riviera, where we found a good berth in one of the many marinas. We telephoned Gerald to let him know we had his boat berthed in a lovely new marina in a very pretty bay. As it was now time for me to collect my first leg back in Roehampton, it was decided that Gerald would come with another pilot in addition to his wife and two children. This would enable Roy and me to fly back, collect my leg and then rejoin the boat, leaving the family to enjoy a little holiday on their boat on their own. The other pilot was an elderly gentleman named Joe Fraser, who was I believe Churchill's last personal pilot. He was delighted to assist as he was keen to keep up his flying hours in order to maintain his licence. He flew quite differently to Gerald. As soon as we were buckled up, Gerald flipped the switches and in no time at all we were airborne. In contrast, Joe checked absolutely everything and certainly took his time before racing down the runway.

It felt very odd to be walking again on two legs. My artificial one felt a little uncomfortable but I soon got used to it. To begin with I had to use both crutches until my leg muscles were strong enough to take the load. It was the norm to wear a form of suspender belt to hold up the stocking that covered the prosthesis, which also helped to keep the leg on. This would not be the answer for me working on a boat. Wearing a suspender belt with a bikini may sound sexy, but for me it was a no-goer. After trying unsuccessfully with a small strap across the knee, it was decided to use a very tight thigh-length stocking over the leg with additional elastic added in the top band, a bit like the ones worn by people suffering from varicose veins. Cosmetically this looked okay, especially after I soaked the stocking in a tea solution so it toned in with the colour of my good leg. I found rolling it down to just above the knee made it even tighter and good for when I was doing any real strenuous leg work. This stopped a lot of the pumping movement within the socket, reducing the problem of chaffing. My fitter also cut the outer leg layer down to fit under the knee rather than over the top. This gave me more freedom of movement, especially when kneeling, and didn't stick out so much when I sat down.

I had always loved dancing, as had my parents. They were great ballroom dancers, and as a young girl, they sent me off to lessons. I wanted to do tap but they insisted I learnt more formal dancing. I have to admit in later years I used to love Dad taking me round the room in a waltz or quickstep. The good news was that my new leg enabled me to still dance, and once I became more confident I could jive and jig along with the best of them. I still had rhythm and was able to apply it. Yeh!

Two weeks later Roy and I were back on the boat, and we continued further up the coast towards Gerald's chosen permanent mooring near Nice. It was lovely not being under any time pressure, and we spent a couple of enjoyable weeks coastal hopping. At one marina we met an interesting chap on an old ketch who was entertaining Valerie Singleton (ex-Blue Peter presenter, a BBC children's programme) and her friend. It ended up being quite a drunken evening. It was then I discovered my leg could float. I was trying to steer Roy in a straight line off the gangway when he toppled overboard, taking me with him. The leg instantly came off, and although I lost the stump sock, the leg bobbed up to the surface close by. Roy immediately sobered up, and with many helping hands we managed to get both of us and my very wet leg back on board the catamaran. I was warned by my fitter that salt water getting into the ankle joint would not be good news, something I was able to confirm later. We finally arrived at our destination, a very pretty marina just south of Nice, and on 14 August we flew back to England in Gerald's Cessna.

Chapter 11 – A Spell Of Yacht Deliveries

Through delivering Gerald's boat, a good contact was made with Reg Smith and his boatyard, Sailcraft, where the catamarans were being built. Roy became their recommended boat delivery skipper for their clients, and it wasn't long before another delivery was booked, this time to Barbados for an English couple. In the meantime we ended up as part of the boatyard's sales team at the Southampton Boat Show in September. Amusingly, Roy managed to clinch one of their better sales. He started to talk to a rather scruffy-looking Midlands chap who the rest of the sales team chose to ignore. Two hours later he had signed up for one of their Cherokee 35 ft catamarans. In his broad Brummie accent, he said he had only come to buy his wife some deck shoes. There were drinks all round that night.

On 14 October we set off on our yacht delivery to Barbados. Once again it was an Apache 40 catamaran. There were six of us on board in total. The owners, Dick and Mary, and two guys Andy and Chris, and of course ourselves. I wouldn't be able to do the whole trip across the Atlantic as my second leg was due to be completed within the next couple of weeks, so I would fly back from Gibraltar. It wasn't exactly en route, but the owners wanted to stop off there before heading across to the Canary Islands.

The weather was pretty grim to begin with, resulting in coastal hopping between the squalls, but by the time we entered the Bay of Biscay the weather had settled down to give us reasonable, if rather sloppy, sailing conditions. The owners had decided it was a good idea not to have a cooker but to rely on just a microwave. This meant that if you wanted a hot drink whilst on night watch, you had to fire up the generator which then woke up the rest of the crew. Crazy or what! Another oddity was that they brought their pet with them. It was an albino polecat – a member of the weasel family, and rather like a ferret – oddly named Puss. He was quite a friendly little thing, so long as you didn't get between him and food. Often we would find him head-first in the rubbish bin, licking food remains from a tin or two. Remarkably he was trained to squat over the self-bailing holes in the cockpit, so no toilet tray was needed. Sadly, I heard later on that he died about halfway across the Atlantic. He had the habit of taking all sorts of things he fancied back to his little nest, and unfortunately this included some seasick pills that he then ate. They had a ceremonial burial at sea. It was perhaps just as well because I don't think the owners had thought about what they were going to do with Puss once they reached the West Indies.

Once we rounded Cape Finisterre the weather started to deteriorate again, and we had to shelter in a small bay tucked behind Cape St Vincent along with half the Spanish fishing fleet. There was no way we would make it through the Straits of Gibraltar. We therefore ran with the wind to Tenerife, arriving on 8 November. Brilliant timing, as we managed to catch up with Ocean Spirit. Les, who had by then left the navy, was taking it over to the West Indies to do some chartering before heading to the States.

I was about to buy my air ticket back to England when Mary came up with a brilliant idea. She found out that the cheapest berth on one of Fred Olsen's cruise ships that happened to be in port was the same price as a flight back. Why not enjoy a three-day cruise back instead? It was due to leave the evening of 11 November at 2300 hours. That evening there was a party on Ocean Spirit. It must have been a good one as I can't remember much about it. All I do know is that I was carried on board Blenheim in a very inebriated state. I came to the following morning, comfortably lying in a double bunk in a rather spacious cabin. Apparently, the purser, who happened to be the only bachelor officer on board, took one look at the state I was in and decided it would be better if I was in one of their first-class cabins. What a lovely man. I have never seen so much food in all my life. Every mealtime the buffet tables were laden, and I was well impressed with the sculptured butter centrepieces. There were so many lovely delicious new things to try. As I was stuffing myself over the next three days, I couldn't help but feel sorry for Roy and the rest of the crew struggling to cook very basic food in that stupid microwave. Fortunately, long cotton dresses were fashionable at that time so I had a couple in my luggage that I rotated wearing in the evenings, which was just as well, especially as I was on the captain's table on two occasions. I was so spoilt. With my short hair, easy clothes and lack of make-up, it didn't take me long to get ready for the evening, so I found myself sitting amongst quite a few charming elderly gentlemen at the bar whilst they waited for their wives to appear. I never had to pay for a single drink. Weirdly, to begin with I became quite dizzy every time I looked out of the side windows. I was just not used to travelling that fast at sea.

By the beginning of December I was the proud owner of two artificial legs, which is what you are allowed on the NHS. As the angle of the foot was fixed, I had to decide on how high a heel I wanted to wear. I was advised by a seasoned female amputee to choose a classic height that would hopefully weather the changes of fashion. My first leg was made for a flat shoe, which was the only sensible thing to do if I was to continue messing about on boats. My dilemma was what to do with my second one. I eventually decided on a one and a half inch heel so that I could dress a little more femininely when I wanted to. Fortunately, short, thick heels were quite fashionable at that time. This also meant I could wear long boots, which were all the rage that winter. The only problem was that if one or the other needed repairs, it would restrict my footwear. This would be particularly problematic if the flat-footed leg broke; wearing heels on a boat is not good news. Luckily, it rarely happened, and the problem was solved a few years later when adjustable ankle joints were introduced.

Whilst I was waiting at home in Ongar for Roy's return from the delivery, having some quiet time on my own, I began to think seriously about my future. I had already come to the conclusion that our time together was not going to be forever. I knew one day I would want to settle down and experience motherhood, and that's when our age difference would matter. Roy had already been through one marriage and having a child, and although we didn't really discuss it, it was obvious he didn't want to settle down to start another family. For me to do this I knew it would mean having to let go of Roy and return to a more normal life, where hopefully I would find someone else to love. But hey, at twenty-three I was in no hurry to do so just yet, and certainly not ready to give up Roy and my somewhat free and easy lifestyle. Not knowing what lay ahead workwise, I began to wonder if I should find a job, even if it was just for a few months before we were off again on another adventure. I was uncomfortable about being financially dependent on Roy, so I decided to look locally. No way did I want to go back to commuting to London. Checking the local paper, I noticed there was a PA (personal assistant) job vacancy at the local branch of May and Bakers, the pharmaceutical chemical company. I applied and got an interview. Whilst waiting in reception, I bumped into an old school friend who worked there. She warned me that the person seeking the PA position was a bully of a man who had lost many an assistant. Braced with this information, I walked into his office with the full intention of not wanting the job, especially as I was still uncertain about committing to staying for any amount of time in Ongar. I was already missing the sea. When he asked about my shorthand speed I told him it was awful, and that he should get with it and use an audio machine. All that did was encourage him to ask about what I had been up to recently. The rest of the interview was spent looking at a map of the world he had on the wall, with me showing him the various sailing routes I had been on. A week later I was offered the job. I think he respected the fact that I wouldn't stand any nonsense from him, and on that basis I believe we would have got on okay.

As it turned out, by then Roy had returned, and we decided to head back down to the coast and stay with our friends Midge and Graham and their four children in Lee-on-Solent. They had a spare downstairs bedroom so we became their lodgers until the following March, which was when our next yacht delivery from Sailcraft was booked in for. It was during this time that England was suffering from numerous mail strikes. Midge had this brilliant idea of setting up a courier business using a minivan. Roy got quite excited about this and agreed to go halves in the business. He paid for the minivan and Midge became the working partner, assisted by me when we were around. Someone came up with 'Femail Couriers', which we all thought was a great name for the company. There were quite a few small industrial business units springing up in the area which we targeted with our canvassing, and in no time Midge found herself travelling all over the place and we started to make a little money.

It was great fun staying with Midge and Graham. Their youngest, David, would pop his head round the bedroom door every day and ask me if my leg had grown back. One night both Roy and I woke up with a start, not knowing why. We then saw our bedroom door starting to open. 'Is that you, David?' said I. Suddenly the door slammed and there were lots of scuffling noises. We realised we were being burgled. Roy jumped out of bed and ran naked up the cul de sac towards the main road, waving my artificial leg as if it were a weapon. The burglar escaped in his car parked close by. Midge and Graham were woken up, and fifteen minutes later we were all sitting in the kitchen with two policemen, armed with mugs of tea, with me retelling the story. Even the policemen had tears of laughter rolling down their faces. It turned out that our house was the last of four that had been burgled that night, including the local mayor's house. All we lost was £5 of Femail Courier's petty cash from the hall bureau.

When you become an amputee you have to resit your driving test. Once I got the hang of making the adjustments needed, I had no problem driving a manual car. Having my artificial leg on the right-hand side made it more of a challenge as the right foot is used for both the brake and the accelerator. Not only had I lost all feeling in the foot, I was also unable to flex the ankle to move the foot up and down. I had to get used to the distance between the pedals when moving the wooden foot from one to the other, and move my whole leg forward for pressing the foot down. I even managed to drive the Lotus Europa without any real problems. I decided to have a couple of driving lessons to eliminate any bad habits such as crossing hands on the steering wheel. Also, I needed a bog-standard car to take the test in. I think any examiner would be reluctant to climb into a somewhat powerful and very low-lying sports car, especially not knowing the driver's capabilities. There may have even been some ruling about it. My instructor was a friendly older guy, and after I impressed him with my driving on the first lesson, he suggested I apply for the test straight away. He did warn me that in my case the test would be twice as long as the examiner would be a lot more thorough before issuing a pass. As I was keen to sort this as soon as possible, I ticked all the towns close by. Just my luck – it ended up being Winchester. Firstly, I wasn't really familiar with the place, and secondly, it had lots of hills. Whilst driving there with my instructor, nerves were beginning to get the better of me; so much so, that just before we entered the town the instructor told me to make a right turn into a pub car park. The small sherry he insisted I drank did the trick. I felt a lot calmer once back behind the wheel. Imagine that happening today with all the drink driving laws. Thankfully, the test went without incident and I passed. The examiner even shook my hand and said it was a pleasure driving with me. How about that! I was well chuffed.

By the beginning of March, Roy was back and forth to Brightlingsea preparing for our next delivery. Once again it was one of their Apache 40 cats, named Aquavit. This time the destination was Newport Beach, California. I was so excited about this trip and couldn't wait to start. By the middle of March, I was in full flow making numerous lists in preparation for provisioning for the long trip. As done in the past, I did a deal with the local cash and carry so that I could buy in bulk, which was quite a cost saving. You were supposed to have a retail business to get a card, but the manager was quite happy to grant me a temporary one once he realised how long the list was. On each boat trip we would fill a watertight canister with some emergency equipment. Apart from a number of additional flares, some of the things we added were fish hooks, string, a

Swiss army knife, suntan lotion, antiseptic cream, some first aid dressings and energy sweets. Hopefully we would have time to throw some tins and water in the life raft.

On Saturday 25 March, 1972, we set sail. This time we had just one other crew member – Mike, a local chap we got to know through Gerald, who lived in Moreton, not far from Ongar. He was about my age, and once again we had a crew member who had no previous sailing experience which, as we knew, suited Roy well. Like Roy, Mike was a laid-back sort of guy who had a great sense of humour and such a wicked laugh. As we were going to be living very close together for many weeks, it was more important that we had someone we felt certain we would get on with and who would willingly pull his own weight. Long-distance sailing is very much a team effort, and with just three of us, it had to work well. Once again the weather was not kind to us. The forecast predicted quite a deep depression heading our way, so we decided to sail into Portsmouth harbour for shelter. We ended up on a mooring off Hardway in Gosport. The wind was so strong we couldn't even row the dinghy ashore to our favourite pub The Jolly Roger. We finally left two days later but had to run for shelter again, this time to Yarmouth in the Isle of Wight. Depressions were rapidly following each other with little break in between. We managed to get to Alderney in the Channel Islands, where we were galebound for a further two days. We finally left early evening on 3 April, but by 0300 the following day the winds increased to a force nine, which left us with no alternative but to turn around and run downwind on bare sticks. We had to clear the Channels Islands before dark that day. We were surfing up to fifteen knots through the Alderney Race which was pretty scary. The Channel Islands are not the place to be in rough weather. So many ships and yachts have been lost in that area over many centuries. It's a sailor's graveyard.

With all three of us utterly exhausted, it was with great relief that we finally entered Cherbourg Harbour in Normandy, France, at 0400 the following morning. It was so demoralising as this took us further back from leaving Portsmouth seven days previously. What a disastrous start to our long trip. We spent the next three days putting the boat back to rights after suffering such a battering, whilst we waited for the weather to improve. Having a cup of tea, listening to yet another depressing weather forecast, we were suddenly aware someone had jumped on board. We were confronted with a tall American guy who was obviously very angry. It was Frank Trane, the owner of the boat. We were so surprised. The plan had been for him to join us in Tenerife so that he could experience sailing his boat across the Atlantic. We had given him an estimated time of arrival, but of course we were well late due to the weather. What we hadn't realised was that the boatyard had promised Frank that we would provide him with regular progress reports. If we had known this, we would have tried to make contact whenever we could but would have explained to Frank before starting the voyage that this was not always possible. If I remember correctly, the ship-to-shore radio range back in the seventies was around twenty to thirty miles from a shore station. The norm was to inform the owner once the destination had been reached. In this case that would have been Tenerife. There is an old saying: 'Boats have destinations but not times of arrival'.

As Frank had not heard anything from us, I believe he had convinced himself that we had stolen his boat. In the process of tracking us down it took him five days of travelling from port to port, carrying a large amount of luggage. That was quite an expensive and challenging exercise. It wasn't until quite recently that I learnt the full story. Apparently, upon arriving in London and discovering the boatyard had no idea where we were, Frank then flew to Lisbon in Portugal. Not finding the boat there, he hired a car and drove to Vigo in Spain, spending one and a half days checking various ports along the way. Someone then told him he reckoned Aquavit was still in the English Channel. Frank then flew to Paris and rented another car, and drove along the coast asking many people if they had seen the boat. Finally someone told him it was in Cherbourg, which was where he found us. Wow! No wonder he wasn't exactly feeling amiable when he came on board. Apart from anything else he must have been exhausted. Fortunately, in true naval fashion, Roy had recorded every weather forecast in the logbook along with our very precise movements. Even then Frank was not fully convinced. Against Roy's better judgement we set sail at 1030 the following day and made it back to Alderney by the afternoon in very heavy rain. Yet another depression then hit us, causing a further three-day delay. Frank was beginning to appreciate what we had been up against. Although the winds were abating, the sea was still very rough. On a broad reach with our sails reefed down, we were surfing the big waves. You could feel the wave pick up the boat, and away you went with your heart in your mouth whilst you wrestled with the steering wheel, trying not to fall off the wave. The speed went off the clock on more than one occasion, which meant we were doing more than twenty knots. The rigging was humming, and knowing how hard we were pushing the boat, we just prayed that Aquavit would not let us down. Being a well-designed catamaran built to a very high standard, we needn't have worried. The hairy sail down the coast of Spain to Vigo must have made Frank realise what heavy weather sailing was all about, and he was full of respect after that. It was the start of a wonderful friendship between us all. At long last the weather and seas started to improve, and we experienced some beautiful downwind sailing heading towards Madeira. After all the crap weather this was pure heaven. There were times when, tied by rope in the galley, struggling to get some soup going in the largest pot to avoid spillage, that I wondered why the hell I was doing this sort of thing. With the better weather I could now feed the crew with something more substantial than just soup. The stress was beginning to melt away, there were smiles on our faces and we all got a little more sleep – yeh!

Madeira is part of Portugal. With its year-round spring-like weather it was a very popular place for the genteel British around the turn of the century, and they certainly left their mark. There were plenty of Victorian-style buildings and many formal gardens, particularly in and around the capital town of Funchal. It was an island of flowers, and listening to the many laid-back Portuguese people singing out loud was very infectious. I found myself walking around with the biggest grin on my face. I really loved the island. One thing that amazed us all was how many old cars there were. You would think that the salt air would have destroyed them many years beforehand. We spent four days there. Poor Aquavit took quite a bashing, especially the trampoline between the two hulls. That needed a great deal of stitching. My left-handed sailmaker's palm earnt its keep, that's for sure. Frank insisted we took one day off to tour the island before we set off to cross 'the pond'. He hired a car with a driver, and when it arrived our mouths dropped open. It was an open-top 3-litre black Bentley complete with running boards, built in the 1920s. It was magnificent. We rode in style, taking in the beauty of the island with its many mountains and lush valleys.

We finally left beautiful Madeira on 25 April – next stop Barbados. What a contrast with the weather. The next few days the winds were very light, and often we were becalmed. We started to go slightly off track to find the elusive trade winds, but finally, on day seven, they returned. All hands were on deck to get the spinnaker flying, and we were away. It was getting warmer and the first of the flying fish were starting to land on deck. When disturbed they take flight, and sometimes one hits the sails and lands on deck. I know in Barbados they eat them, but for most they are too bony and not worth the effort. On day ten we had a torrential rain shower, which was welcome as we all got to have a freshwater shower on deck. All in all, it wasn't a bad crossing. We had the odd squall and some light winds but mostly steady trade-wind sailing. It took seventeen days, arriving in Barbados on 12 May – in the dark, of course. We spent four lovely days in Barbados. Frank was very generous, wining and dining us ashore, and we all slept well. By the time we left, not only the boat's batteries but our own were fully charged up. Next stop was my beloved Bequia. I couldn't wait to return. One and a half days later found us dropping our anchor in Port Elizabeth bay, and just for a change it was daylight. Sitting under the bougainvillea at the Frangipani, sipping a rum punch, was so, so heavenly. It was a worthy reward after battling though some pretty awful weather at the start of our trip. We had arrived in the middle of the Bequia–St Vincent races, so the island was buzzing. It was such a contrast to the quiet of being at sea and took a little time to get used to. Cutty Sark was constantly heard being shouted whenever any Bequians recognised us. When we told Frank all about how we won the race two years previously, he was keen to see if we could join the race back to St Vincent. We managed to get permission and – surprise, surprise – we won! Apache 40s are fast sailing boats. and of course Roy was one of the best skippers. Frank was ecstatic. The prize-giving, as usual, was at the Mariners Inn which is opposite Young Island. Although we weren't entitled to any prize, at the end of the prize-giving I was handed a magnum of champagne as a welcome back to St Vincent. Wow – what a truly wonderful thing to happen. I was overwhelmed with emotion, and the memories of the accident came flooding back along with all the compassion from so many Vincentians. What a night of celebration we had, reunited with all our chums who were still living out there.

Frank had arranged for some friends and his wife, Allan, to join us whilst we very slowly worked our way through the islands towards St Thomas in the US Virgin Islands. Allan and the first two couples arrived the following day, and what a relaxing time we all had sailing to St Lucia, Martinique, Dominique, Guadeloupe and Antigua, and being wined and dined in a grand way in many places en route. In contrast to Frank, Allan was quite a reserved lady and a lot calmer by nature. Both Roy and I liked her a lot. In Antigua the two couples left, and two other couples joined us for the leg to St Thomas. And so the leisurely sailing, wining and dining continued throughout the British and US Virgin Islands. We were being thoroughly spoilt to the point we were getting used to such a luxurious way of life. Frank and Allan were leaving us at St Thomas, and they decided we must go to the best restaurant there was before departing. We headed to Bluebeard's Castle in our smartest clothes, only to find that the gentlemen had to wear jackets. For goodness sake, we were in the West Indies. They had a rack of jackets that you could hire for the evening, but Frank wasn't having any of it. If his smart silk shirt was not good enough for them, they didn't deserve our custom, so we went to another restaurant where Frank spent a small fortune on food and drinks for us all. Bluebeard's loss!

Chapter 12 – California Here We Come

On 14 June we set sail again on what we regarded as Phase III of the trip. Panama Canal, here we come. In most ports you will find guys wanting to work their way on a boat to somewhere or other. So, in St Thomas an English chap called Peter joined us, along with an old friend Jo – an English girl who used to be married to one of the yacht skippers and was keen to experience taking a yacht through the canal. It made a nice change to have another girl on board. We pressed on with little stopping as Roy was anxious to get into the Pacific. We were now into the start of the hurricane season, and each day we could feel the temperature rising as we sailed closer towards the equator. We had some fantastic days of sailing and were often escorted by lots of dolphins.

On 19 June, just a day away from the Panama Canal, the weather changed dramatically. The winds increased and there was plenty of heavy rain. With the storm came bolts of lightning which hit the surrounding sea. I got so anxious that I took off my watch; I didn't want to have anything metal on me. The heavy rain caused very poor visibility, and being in the approach zone of the canal we were aware that there were many huge ships close by. Would they detect our little radar reflector on the top of our mast? We felt extremely vulnerable. As it was getting dark, Roy made the decision not to continue heading towards the canal. Instead we spent the whole night sails down with the engine on, motoring back and forth, hopefully in an area clear of shipping. None of us slept that night. As soon as dawn arrived, we changed course and headed straight for the canal, arriving in the holding area later that morning. By then the storm had passed through. A pilot boat greeted us, and we were told to tie up to a huge buoy, joining two other yachts. We then discovered we had been caught in the tail end of a hurricane and that it had destroyed part of the marina, smashing the boats up on the shore. What luck that we had just managed to miss it. The other two boats had arrived just before us, so we were all feeling very relieved. Sadly, because of all the damage to the marina, we couldn't get ashore, leaving us all stranded in the middle of the waiting area whilst the mass of paperwork was cleared for us to proceed through the canal. The fee for each vessel, whether it was a supertanker or a small sailing yacht, was worked out by volume, which involved some time-consuming measuring. What a crazy way of doing it, especially for the yachts. It would have been far easier just to set a fixed fee as the difference in cost between each boat must have been miniscule. All this took a couple of frustrating days, leaving us little to do but swelter in the hot climate. Swimming was out of the question as the water was quite polluted.

Whilst hanging around, a crew member from one of the other boats asked if I was Terri. 'Yes,' said I, 'but I don't think we have met.'

'No, you don't know me,' he said, 'but you do know my girlfriend. She told me all about your accident – she was the nurse that looked after you.'

'Oh my God, not Frankie!' I squealed. I could not believe it. What a coincidence, and what was more, they lived in Newport Beach, which was our destination. Emotions got the better of me and I started to cry. I never thought I would be able to thank her properly, and now I could. Frankie had given up nursing and was working as cabin crew with United Airlines. He gave me their contact details, along with the plan that once we all arrived in California we would arrange to meet up. What a truly small world it is!

On 24 June we were boarded by a rather rude pilot who claimed he hated taking yachts through the canal and assumed we would feed him lunch. I believe the Panama Canal is the only place where the pilot takes charge of the vessel instead of the captain. In no time at all we found ourselves in the first set of locks. There are three locks that took us up to Gatun Lake and then another three dropping us down into the Pacific. It was a good job there were five of us on board as it needed one crew member on each of the four corners of the boat, keeping each rope taut at all times whether going up or coming down. The locks are huge and the rush of water that surges in could easily destroy a yacht if not under control. Going up you pull the ropes in and going down you let them out. I'm not sure what was hardest; pulling them in was physically tough, but letting them out needed full concentration to make sure you did not end up with a winding turn. That's when one turn of the rope jams underneath another. The rope will then need to be slackened off to unjam it – potentially disastrous if it happened in those locks, so Roy was ready with spare rope just in case. All of this was being done in very hot conditions, and it was impossible to pause for even a second. For the ships, small motorised trucks moved alongside the canal, moving the ropes from one set of locks to the next as the vessel was moved along. This couldn't be done with yachts, so some poor chaps had to run with the ropes instead, going up and down the little hillocks that separated each lock.

We were absolutely exhausted and dripping wet by the time

we came through the three sets of locks going up into Gatun Lake, and we asked if we could pause by anchoring in one of the beautiful little inlets to rest whilst having lunch. We could see quite a few Panamanian Indians paddling their canoes and would have loved to have got a little closer to them, but no, our very unfriendly pilot insisted we continued on and have lunch on the go. Such a shame, as we heard later that some pilots did allow this and also included a welcome swim to cool off. So, we continued on to the downward flights, and thankfully with no mishaps we soon found ourselves safely through the canal into the Pacific Ocean. In his hurry to get off our boat, the pilot left his hat behind. We were not at all sorry. We then turned to starboard and headed up the coast of Costa Rica, whilst I longingly looked to port in the direction of all the beautiful and romantic Pacific islands. Having recently read Aku Aku by Thor Heyerdahl, I so wanted to visit Easter Island. Hey ho, perhaps one day I will.

We had a beautiful sail all the way up the Costa Rican coast, arriving at our next stop, Corinto, in Nicaragua, on 28 June. What a crazy reception we had. As normal, we dropped anchor in the harbour, flying our 'Q' flag. In no time at all we spotted a small motorised dinghy approaching. In it were crammed four black gentlemen, with one very large, very old white man standing up in the centre. Coming alongside, the elderly white gentleman greeted us with a 'Heil Hitler' salute and gave us an enormous wink. We just didn't know what to think of it and daren't laugh in case we offended him. Dealing with customs and immigration people is never a joke. We were told to bring the yacht alongside the town quay where clearance would be done. We reckoned the reason for this was that the guy would have found it difficult to climb on board from the dinghy.

By the time we tied up to the dock, quite a large crowd of people had come to watch, so this rather interesting white man left his entourage on the dock and suggested we went down below. When he discovered we were British (the boat was flying the US flag), he insisted on having tea. So there we were, sipping tea in a baking hot cabin, politely making conversation. He told us he was in the Black Watch Regiment in the First World War and lived for a while in London. He mentioned a friend's name who still lived there and asked if we happened to know him. So bizarre! Paperwork was eventually completed, but he insisted in taking away our passports for photocopying. This made us very nervous. Nicaragua wasn't exactly the most politically stable country back then, and there was no indication as to when we could leave. The only reason we stopped in Corinto in the first place was because we were almost out of water and fuel and needed some fresh produce as we hadn't been able to go ashore in Panama. Before the boat was completed, one of the last things Frank asked the yard to install was a water filter system. This was a huge benefit as we didn't need to worry about storing and paying for bottled water. We were also able to wash all fresh produce easily. It took three days to get our passports back. Each day Roy would walk up the hill to the customs office, and it wasn't until he took up some copies of Playboy we happened to have on board that our passports were returned. He had noticed the old boy had roving eyes when it came to Jo and me.

With great relief we shook the sails free and soon found ourselves on a broad reach heading towards Acapulco in Mexico. On this leg of the trip there was so much wildlife. Each day we would have an escort of dolphins. I used to lay flat on my stomach on the trampoline and watch them dipping and diving between the two hulls. Just off the starboard hull a small group of young dolphins were following along. Every now and again one of them would head towards the boat to join in the fun, but one of the adults would quickly nudge it back to the young group. I was amazed and felt very privileged to have witnessed this. It was plain to see that the adults felt the game was too dangerous for the children. As the dolphins passed under the trampoline I was able to touch them, and what a thrill it was when one or two of them rolled over for me to touch their tummies. Such a truly awesome experience, and one I will never forget.

By 1000, if we wanted fish that day, then not only did we catch one by then, but we could afford to be choosy. Dorado, or dolphin as we called it, was still our favourite. On one occasion we saw two killer whales playing together; or were they fighting? Most of their bodies were out of the water and they were twirling around together. This went on for quite some time. It was fantastic to watch, but I was quite relieved it was not too close to the boat. We must have passed twenty to thirty copulating turtles, each couple at a distance from the next and all in a row, about a mile or so offshore. Extraordinary. In some bays we could see lots of seals. There were so many in one that we decided to do a detour and sail in. As we swept around the bay, all the females and pups left the beach leaving only the bulls to guard their own family area, barking furiously. We kept seeing the female seals pop their heads up close to the boat, full of curiosity. They reminded me of Labrador dogs.

We didn't stay long in Acapulco. As it was a city, we didn't feel it was safe to leave the boat unattended. Such a contrast to the poor canning hamlets further back along the coast where we felt so much more at ease when returning their friendly waves. Also, by then I was having trouble with my prosthesis. I had to take it off as the bottom of my stump developed blisters and was really sore. We were told there was a good limb-fitting centre in Puerto Vallarta, so after filling up with water and grabbing a few provisions, we were soon back at sea. It was a real pain dealing with customs and immigration in Mexico, and I hope things have improved since the seventies. In most countries, once you have cleared into one port you are then able to stop off anywhere in that country. Not so Mexico. Every time you stop at a port you have to go through the rigmarole of clearing each time, and as they require all forms to be completed in Spanish in triplicate, it becomes necessary to make use of a local agent, and of course this does not come cheap.

We arrived in Puerto Vallarta on 8 July, which was where Jo left us. A friend had been looking after her little girl, and it was time she returned to being a mummy again. We managed to locate the limb-fitting centre, and I was delighted to meet two ex-Roehampton chaps who were working there. My prosthesis really interested them as they had not seen one cut down to fitting under the knee before. My fitter back in Roehampton had been quite revolutionary with the design. They soon diagnosed the problem. My stump had lost a little weight and therefore the bottom of it was touching the base of the socket, which is a big no-no. It should be supported by the sides, leaving some air space at the bottom. They squirted in some foam and five minutes later I was walking again. Such a relief. When something like that happens it pulls me up short, reminding me of my vulnerability, and I hate it. We had to pay something, but it was a minimal amount thanks to the guys. Puerto Vallarta was so much better than Acapulco, and it was great to sample some real Mexican food.

One evening shortly after leaving Puerto Vallarta, I was messing with the radio whilst on watch and managed to tune into an American station. I got so excited at the thought of nearing the end of our voyage that I decided to open a bottle of margarita to celebrate. Little did I realize how potent a mix it was. It was my very tuneless singing along to a pop song that brought Roy up on deck. By then, most of the bottle had been consumed, and one very inebriated and definitely legless girl was promptly steered below and put to bed. I had one hell of a hangover the following morning, and to this day I cannot stomach tequila.

Frank joined us in Ensenada so he would be on board when we cleared ourselves into the US. Five days after leaving Puerto Vallarta we arrived in San Diego. I always like to arrive in port with the boat in shipshape order and this was no exception. Knowing how strict US customs and immigration were, we made sure we had no half-full bottles of booze left, and ate up the last of the fresh food. We then braced ourselves for the ordeal, and boy, what an ordeal we had. It took two days to clear us. The first thing they did was put a dog on board as they had the opinion that every boat coming from Mexico would be carrying drugs. Because of the distance we had travelled, every single piece of paperwork from every country visited was minutely scrutinised. Thank goodness we had Frank on board to tackle the many questions asked before we were finally cleared to proceed to our final destination – Newport Beach. During clearance, Jo, with her little girl, arrived to welcome us to the US. As we were not allowed ashore, all conversation between us had to be from a distance with Jo standing on the customs dock. By the time we were allowed ashore, only a short amount of time was spent together as Jo had to return home. That was the last time I saw her. Sadly, a few years later she had a paragliding accident that left her paralysed from the waist down. It was also here that our other crew member Peter left us. So now we were down to the original three – Mike, Roy and myself – and, of course, Frank.

On 20 July 1972 we finally arrived in Newport Beach, almost four months since leaving the Essex coast back in England. Before reaching our final destination we decided to top up with diesel at the fuel dock. Shortly after arriving we received a very excited visitor. It was the film actor Buddy Ebsen, famous for his role as Jed in The Beverly Hillbillies. He had been sitting in his panoramic-view sitting room and spotted us arriving in the bay. Being an enthusiastic catamaran sailor, he loved the look of our boat but didn't recognise the make. He did no more than jump in his car and drive round the bay to find us. There were very few large catamarans in that part of California, hence the reason why Frank went to all the trouble of buying one in the UK. We gave him the grand tour and he went away feeling very envious of Frank's new toy, and promised to get his secretary to fix a date for us to have a personal tour of the studios, which I was really looking forward to.

Frank and his wife, Allan, had a beautiful house. It used to be Shirley Temple's beach house and came complete with its own beach – the sand had been shipped in. Needless to say, the interior was straight out of one of the glossy magazines. Elegant subtle colours with beautiful, expensive pieces of antique furniture. There was a cabinet displaying some artefacts, one of which was a wooden horse from the Tutankhamun tomb. And what a luxury it was to sleep in one of their spacious guest bedrooms. I remember the first morning there. Gasping for a cup of tea, I went downstairs to the kitchen. It was still early so no one else was up. I started opening some cupboards to locate a mug and was startled to find a large cupboard full of an antique silver dinner service for about thirty. Wow!

We spent the next two days scrubbing and cleaning the boat. I remember at one stage feeling exceptionally hot. I decided to dive overboard for a swim and got quite a shock. Although the weather was beautifully hot, the water temperature was decidedly cooler. A few days after arriving Frank and Allan hosted a boat-welcoming party. There were quite a few of their friends, including the four couples who had joined us for part of the trip. Lasagne was all the rage then, so that was what we had served on the beautiful antique silver dinner service previously spotted. The day after the party Buddy Ebsen's secretary called with a date for the studio tour, but we had to decline as it clashed with a dinner date we had already accepted from one of the couples at the party. I was really disappointed about this, and even more so when, just a couple of hours before we were due to go, it was cancelled due to the lady having a headache. Grrr! One of the first things I did when we arrived was to contact Frankie, the nurse. She was about to go off on a work flight, but we arranged to meet five days later. That was such a special day. We met her and her boyfriend at a fish restaurant for lunch and spent virtually the rest of the day there. We hugged and chatted, and she was very impressed with how well I walked. I was so pleased that at long last I could properly thank her for all she did for me back in the Grenadines the previous year.

Newport Beach is a very impressive upmarket area of California. Frank and Allan had quite a lifestyle. Frank was an extremely active person and had a passion for surfing. Most mornings he would be up and out early, heading for one of the many surf beaches in the area. He had a small motorhome which was bought just so he could have a shower at the beach before returning home, and of course it was a top quality one. Frank owned a land development company, and once a month his general manager, Joe, would fly down to Newport Beach. Frank would meet him at the airport in his motorhome, and whilst sitting on their surfboards waiting to catch the big waves, they would discuss company business. After their surfing session, the necessary paperwork would be completed in the motorhome and then Jo would be taken back to the airport. What a way to work.

Allan, on the other hand, was not such an early riser. In the morning after breakfast she would discuss the day's menu and tasks with the housekeeper before preparing herself for whatever social event she had on that day. On one occasion

Allan took me to Cocos for brunch, and I found it amusing when I read about it later that week in the local rag: 'Allan Trane was seen having brunch in Cocos with her English friend Terri'. Allan loved my accent and was forever correcting herself to pronounce words the English way. Frank and Allan had two daughters and a son – a lovely family. Mike got on really well with their eldest daughter.

We stayed with the Tranes for about two weeks. Before leaving, Allan invited me to join her and two of her girlfriends to go to the amphitheatre in Los Angeles to see Jesus Christ Superstar. I had to borrow one of their eldest daughter's dresses as I didn't have any smart clothes with me. None of the girls, including Allan, was keen to drive, so I said I would be happy to so long as I was directed as to where to go. So, not used to driving on the right, before I realised it I found myself sat behind the wheel of a very smart Cadillac, heading towards Los Angeles. Once I hit the six-lane freeway I soon understood why the rest of the party were reluctant to drive. Dad teaching me to drive in the London rush hour did at least help quell the quiet panic that was going on in my head. With relief we arrived at our destination safe and sound, with one very expensive car thankfully still in one piece.

Wow, what a place! The open-air theatre sat up on a hill, with the lights of Beverly Hills and Los Angeles below us. We were surrounded by large speakers mounted on high platforms, and when the music started I was totally blown away. It was the first time I heard any of Andrew Lloyd Webber's music, and ever since it has become a great love of mine. Jesus Christ Superstar will always be my favourite, and every time I hear any of its music, it takes me right back to that amphitheatre. It really was pure magic, and I am so grateful to Allan for taking me along to see it.

Whilst in the States, we decided to catch up with a few

friends. We flew up to New Jersey and stayed with our very first charterers, Bob and Eleanor Harris. Such a lovely couple, who welcomed us with open arms. They lived in a very pleasant suburban area and looked after us so well. On my birthday Roy and I took the train to New York and met up with Roger and Peg, the couple who looked after me in Barbados after my accident. They had an impressive apartment in central New York, and we celebrated my twenty-fourth in style – champagne all the way whilst we explored the clubs and bars around Times Square. What a night. By the third week in September we were heading back to England, without a clue as to what we were going to do next.

Chapter 13 – A Taste of Powerboating

Once again we stayed with our friends Midge and Graham. This meant that Roy could start putting out feelers to find out if there was a delivery coming up or some sort of skipper's job. It was handy staying in Lee-on-Solent as it was very central to the yachting world in the south, being just across the bay from Portsmouth. In the meantime I was able to give Midge a hand around the house and look after the kids whilst she continued running the Femail Courier business. Apart from doing a short delivery of a Westerly 32 from the Solent to the Essex coast in bitterly cold weather, all was quiet on the job front. So, we enjoyed our time out catching up with lots of friends around the country. Before we knew it, it was Christmas, which we spent with my mum and dad. January and February seemed to just fly by, but then, at the beginning of March, Roy heard about a skipper's job available on an 80 ft powerboat that was in the process of being completed in a boatyard in Strood, Kent, on the banks of the Medway. Neither of us were exactly keen to work on a 'stinkpot', but as there didn't seem to be a lot else available, Roy decided to follow it up. The owner was Bob Okin, an attorney from New York. It wasn't long before arrangements were made for Roy to meet with Bob at the boatyard. Roy got the job, and the good news was that the owner was hoping to employ a couple, so I too was included, and it came with a very acceptable joint salary. We had a second meeting with Bob in London so that he could meet me before heading back to New York. We had a very nice meal at the Inn on the Park, and then ended up in a casino. Bob loved to gamble and introduced me to blackjack. Oh boy, did I love that! I took to the game like a duck takes to water. It was great fun, but perhaps not such a good idea, as I was to discover later on.

As Kent was not far from Essex, we moved back to Mum and Dad's. Once I got used to the idea of working on a powerboat, I was really looking forward to the change. It would be a lot more comfortable to live on, and most certainly would include a far better galley than I was used to. I couldn't wait to see the boat. But when I did, my face dropped. I was expecting to see eighty feet of beautiful sleek lines, instead of which I was looking at a very ugly, boxy affair. There was just no style at all. What a disappointment. There were three being built – two 80-footers, named Atlast, which was our one and Laurie Nan and one 120-footer, named Sybarite. All three owners were friends. Just to add insult to injury, the boatyard was a scruffy-looking place, and Strood was a semi-depressed area. All very disheartening.

With a heavy heart I clambered on board to see how much of the fitting out had been done and what was left to do. I felt a little happier when I saw how much space there was in the saloon, and when I stepped into the galley I couldn't stop smiling. There was plenty of counter space, and low and behold there was an American full-size cooker, a dishwasher and an amazing American fridge/freezer complete with a cold-water dispenser that also produced ice. In 1972 this was quite something. There was also a microwave and a garbage compacter, which I had never come across before. After reading the instructions I was amazed at what it could do. Once the bin was full of rubbish – including cans and bottles – at the press of a button a metal plate would come down and crush everything to a very low level, allowing you then to fill the bin again and repeat the performance. There was just one pitfall as I discovered later. Once the bin was at full capacity, even the mighty crusher couldn't reduce it down any more – try lifting the bloody thing! It needed two hefty guys to move it, yet alone upend it into a larger bin ashore.

To begin with, we commuted from Ongar to Strood, which soon became tedious. It took two weeks before we managed to find a room to rent close to the boatyard: a right tatty place, but by then we were beginning to get desperate. As it turned out it was not for long. Just a few weeks later the owners were tipped off that the receivers were about to descend on the boatyard. Those guys moved fast. Within twenty-four hours they managed to hire road transporters to move all three boats out of the yard and take them to a boatyard in East Cowes on the Isle of Wight. When we heard the news, I whooped with glee. Goodbye grotty Strood, hello lovely Cowes, where we had friends and would be right in the thick of it come Cowes Racing Week, which happens every year towards the end of August. Oh, yes!

For the next couple of weeks we stayed with friends on the Isle of Wight who lived close by the boatyard, before we managed to get the men to sort out one of the cabins and some temporary electrics so that we could move on board. By this time we were well into May, and the sailing season had started. We had quite an idyllic time. Roy's main job was to monitor progress and report back to Bob – not a lot of pressure at all. My job was to try and keep the builder's mess down to a minimum, purely to make our life living on board a little more acceptable. It was the same routine for Kev and Marg on Laurie Nan. We didn't do too much socialising with them as they were not really our type of people. They were an odd couple, well into in their forties, who came from somewhere up north. Kev was a large man who was fond of telling stories that didn't quite seem credible. Roy and I definitely got the impression he was a bit of a con man, especially as he avoided any talk regarding his past sailing experience. He certainly loved his beer and had a belly to prove it. Marg, who was no beauty, bless her, was quite content to let Kev do all the talking while she got on with the cooking and cleaning.

As requested by Bob, I started to make lists of all the smaller items needed – kitchen utensils, bed linen and so on – including costs, in preparation for his approval for me to purchase. Once full electrics were installed to the galley I was able to cook, and we did quite a lot of entertaining in a somewhat rustic way, which included looking after Bob when he visited. As he was Jewish and diabetic, I had to think carefully what to feed him. It was during this time that my sister married Richard. Both my younger sister Karen and myself were bridesmaids, so this involved a couple of visits home as Mum, of course, was making all the dresses. It was a truly lovely wedding and a great opportunity to catch up with all the extended family, but I was a little disappointed that Roy was not with me. He said he wasn't into weddings, and opted to remain on board. Understanding him only too well, I didn't try to persuade him otherwise; and anyway, as compensation I got to drive the Lotus Europa home The fun summer drifted into autumn, and before we knew it Christmas was upon us once again. This time we spent it on board, and now the galley was fully operational I was able to cook a huge turkey lunch for friends who, like us, were not with family, and a good time was had by all. Over the next nine months, slowly but surely the boat started to take shape, and it was a welcome sight seeing the wooden panelling being fitted once all the electrics and pipework were completed.

During our time on the Isle of Wight, Roy sold the white Europa and bought a bright red Lotus 2+2S. I absolutely loved that car and had such fun driving it. It was a real head-turner. One weekend I decided to drive home in it. Apart from wanting to see my mum and dad, I was keen to show off the car. In those days the M25 had not been built, so to get from Hampshire to Essex you drove through the centre of London. Coming off the Embankment and heading towards the Corn Exchange in the City, there were some traffic lights ahead. Moving my foot from the accelerator to the brake I misjudged the distance, and it managed to jam between both pedals, resulting in half accelerating and half braking but still moving forward at an alarming rate. All I could do was hit the horn to warn those in front waiting for the lights to change to green, and pull like mad on the handbrake. Fortunately, the lights changed just in time for the cars to move away from me, and the handbrake was good enough to stop the car even though it was still revving a little. I hit the hazard button, then took off my leg and bent down to yank it free, whilst traffic passed me on both sides. I put the leg back on loosely, and managed to manoeuvre the car through the lights and park safely a few yards down the road. Once I stopped shaking from the scare, I got out of the car and pulled up the stocking to properly hold my leg in place. Wearing a miniskirt made it impossible to do it discreetly. Needless to say, I got a couple of wolf whistles! Lesson learnt. From then onwards I always gave myself plenty of time to slow down before needing to stop.

Whilst having supper at the Holmwood hotel with a large group of friends during Cowes Week, I heard my name being yelled. It came from a group of racing guys. I went over to them and discovered the person shouting was Andy, whom I vaguely knew. He was a thalidomide victim, born minus one and a half legs. Someone had obviously told him of my much smaller loss. When we discovered we shared the same doctor up at Roehampton a promise was made to go there together, if and when we both needed repairs done. Messing about with boats, it wasn't long before we both had to go. The metal parts in ankle joints do not like salt water. Andy had one of those hand-control cars so he was the driver. I'm afraid we caused havoc at Roehampton. It all started with our dear Doctor Fletcher introducing us to a young lad who was just getting over an accident and had the same amputation as me. He was so depressed, mostly because he thought he would never be able to drive again, yet alone walk. Both Andy and I promptly told him that was rubbish and firmly assured him that of course he could. As it was close to lunchtime, and both Andy and I knew that our repairs would not be completed for a while yet, using our backup legs to walk we gathered up not only this young chap but quite a few others who were waiting around, including a couple of wheelchair jobs, and staggered up the road to the pub. We must have been quite a sight to passers-by. And that was where the fitters found us merry limbless lot! One or two who remained in the waiting area said it was hilarious seeing their puzzled faces when they came out from their workshop to find most of their patients missing. Both Andy and I got the wagging finger from Dr Fletcher, and we felt like two naughty children. But we achieved our mission of cheering up the young lad, and I think we made a few other patients happy as well.

By September 1974, Atlast was almost completed. Bob's girlfriend Ruby, back in Florida, was given the job of interior designer and providing the furnishings and floor coverings. Oh my God, Roy and I couldn't believe the choice of carpeting. Each of the four cabins had a different colour – orange, light blue, green, and yellow for the master, which was then continued into the lounge. And it was all shag. It was just too much, even for the seventies, especially on a boat. I then had the task of having to colour-match the bed linen for each of the cabins. The other two boats, Laurie Nan and the larger one, Sybarite, kept to the traditional red, white and blue colours. I was so envious, and even though we didn't own the boat, was embarrassed to hear so many negative comments regarding the colour scheme from both the workers and any visitors. When I asked Bob about tableware he told me that his friend, the owner of Sybarite, was providing all of that as a gift. A large box marked 'Melaware' soon arrived, and I had to smile when it was unpacked. There was everything needed for a twelve-place setting in an attractive red, white and blue boat design – totally clashing with the Atlast colour scheme.

Sybarite was the first of the three boats that the original yard in Strood had started work on and consequently was a little more advanced with the fitting out. She was therefore the first boat to start sea trials. By this time it was August, and off she went for her first and, as it turned out, only sea trip. It was discovered that at least one of her stabilisers had only been tack welded, resulting in it coming away as soon as the boat hit some swells. It sank. What a disaster ... or was it? The captain and mate managed to get ashore in the dinghy without any problems and didn't appear to be shaken up by the incident when we spoke to them afterwards. The guys always did keep their distance from the rest of us and avoided any socialising. We felt very suspicious about it all. Needless to say, all welds were carefully checked on both Atlast and Laurie Nan, and thankfully all were found to be good and sound.

Near the end of September Roy took Atlast out for a final sea trail. Mike Whitaker, a friend of ours who was also a professional skipper, came with us to help Roy swing the compass. Mike spent a lot of the time behind the wheel, which turned out to be fortuitous. Both boats were being transported to Florida in the hull of a merchant ship. Part of the ship's hull is flooded, allowing each boat to motor into the vast area. As the water is being pumped out, the ship's crew get busy chocking up and securing each boat. Once all the water has gone, the back of the ship is then closed and secured, and away she steams. All this was scheduled to happen the following Wednesday, 2 October. We worked hard for the next few days, cleaning the boat inside and out and making sure everything was properly secure in readiness for the crossing. Roy was going with the boat, but I was to fly out a few weeks later. Bob had already sent me my flight ticket from Heathrow to Miami.

A farewell party was arranged for the night before departure at our favourite pub, where many of our new and old friends joined us. It wasn't long before Roy became a very happy man with a big grin on his face, surrounded by plenty of mates buying him drinks. Well into the evening, with Roy in a very drunken state, we got word that the ship had arrived, and due to the tides the captain wanted the boats brought into the hull that evening rather than wait for the morning. Bloody hell, thought I, no way was Roy fit to drive the boat, but knowing him, he wouldn't think that. In his mind he would be convinced he was perfectly able to do it. I was only just about okay myself. I was in a state of panic wondering how the hell to deal with this, when in walked Mike, who was fortunately stone cold sober having just arrived from the mainland. After a quick discussion with Mike and a few of the more sober friends, it was decided to hoodwink Roy by telling him the party was continuing on the boat. He readily went along with this once he knew the lady he was chatting up was also coming. Once I explained to her what was going on, she agreed to distract Roy by keeping him down below whilst Mike drove the boat. The others present could then help me with the deck work.

That poor lady. Every now again she would stagger up on deck looking very dishevelled and ask how much longer, and each time we hurriedly sent her back down below. Mike did a wonderful job manoeuvring Atlast into the hull of the ship. We then had to throw a number of ropes to the ship's crew, securing each one to practically every cleat on board. Needing one extra secure point at the bow, I wrapped a rope round the windlass and then ran to the other side to handle yet another rope. All of a sudden I heard the rattle of chain, and to my horror I realised the pressure of the rope around the windlass had released the brake. I remembered Roy had been greasing it the day before, and he must have forgotten to tighten it. Before I could get back to the windlass, there was an almighty clunk as the anchor hit the bottom of the ship's hull. Everyone stopped as the noise vibrated around the ship. And then over the tannoy came the captain's voice speaking in English but with a strong German accent: 'It izz not necessary to drop one's anchor!' I was mortified and felt so very stupid, and of course everyone roared with laughter. At that moment I wished above all else that I was anywhere other than standing on the bow of such an ugly boat, and I was well fed up with Roy allowing himself to get so horribly drunk. What a shambles, and what a low opinion the captain and crew of that ship must have had of us so-called professional sailors.

I had just enough time to write a quick farewell note to Roy, who had by then fallen asleep. That poor lady deserved a medal. I threw the last of my things into my case and, covering Roy with the duvet, kissed him goodbye. Boy, was he going to have a hangover in the morning, and when he came to he would be wondering where the hell he was. By then I was being called to leave the boat. We walked through the ship to a gangway where there was a launch waiting to take us all back to shore.

That night I stayed with friends and caught an early ferry the following morning to the mainland. Just two weeks beforehand, Roy had sold the Lotus. A chap came along and made him such a good offer that Roy would have been foolish to turn it down, especially as we were not sure when we would be returning to England. As I sat on the train heading towards London, I felt quite sad. It was such a pity the way things had turned out. I hated that Roy got himself so very drunk, and although this time it turned out to be an advantage, his desire for another woman whilst in this state was something I was finding harder and harder to accept. I also was very cross that we were given such a late change to the schedule. As tide tables are always available beforehand, the captain could have easily given us more notice. Roy was an excellent skipper, but some people wouldn't believe this, especially the crew of that ship, and Kev and Marg from Laurie Nan with the guys they had on board. I also felt sad that we didn't have the opportunity to say goodbye.

The next couple of weeks were spent relaxing at home, enjoying Mum's good cooking, and in no time at all I was checking in at Heathrow Airport. All went smoothly until I reached immigration at Miami. I had an indefinite multiple-entry US visa, which meant I could come and go to the States as many times as I wanted for up to six months per visit. Just before I left home, I received a phone call from Bob saying I was not to mention that I was joining Atlast as he didn't want to draw any unnecessary attention to the boat. I guessed he was trying to convince the tax man that the boat was second-hand, or something similar. In order to stick as close as possible to the truth, I put Bahia Mar Hotel, Fort Lauderdale, as my address. Bahia Mar Marina was where Atlast was going to be based. When the immigration officer asked me how long I was going to be staying, I stupidly told the truth by stating that I wasn't sure – maybe two or three months. Wearing jeans instead of smarter clothes was also a big mistake. Back in the seventies they were still regarded as working men's clothes and therefore not the norm for travelling, especially in America where they were well behind UK fashions. I was immediately sent to a crowded non-air-conditioned room that was mostly full of Cubans.

It was a good hour or so before I was summoned to be interrogated. By then I was quite concerned. I knew Roy would be waiting in arrivals, but there was no way I could let him know that I was in the airport but delayed at immigration. No mobile phones back then. Why is it that even now a lot of custom and immigration officers in America act so unwelcoming and can sometimes be quite rude? The first question the officer asked me was how much cash I was carrying. I can't remember the amount, but I do know it was not a lot. My defence was that I didn't like to carry too much, being a single girl travelling on my own, which was true. I didn't have a credit or debit card in those days – not many did – but I said I had my cheque book and could easily draw out money at a Barclay's branch as and when I needed it. He then asked me why a Bob Okin from New York supplied the ticket. That threw me. With my mind racing I came up with the story that he was a friend of the family and that it worked out cheaper for him to get the ticket from his travel agent in New York. I felt quite pleased with my reply. He then asked me if I intended to see him. 'No,' said I, 'he is older and is more of a friend of my parents.' After staring at me for a lot longer than I felt comfortable with, he eventually stamped my passport, but then had the audacity to say that he believed I was an international prostitute but had no proof. I was shocked and angry, and said, 'To be quite honest, the appalling way I have been treated since arriving in this country makes me want to catch the next flight home.'

'You just do that,' was his reply, and then he handed me back my passport. I was furious.

From there I had to run the gauntlet of customs, and of

course I was picked out to have my case searched. I'm sure they must have been tipped off by immigration. They started to pull everything out of my case, and when they began to undo the Christmas presents from my mum and dad, with tears in my eyes I said, 'They are presents from my parents, and as I do not want to see what they are, I'm going to turn my back and trust that you will rewrap them and put everything back in my case.' I think I made them feel guilty as it wasn't long before everything was back in place and I was told I could go. I was so upset by the ordeal. All I wanted was to see Roy in arrivals and have a big hug, but of course I was so late he was nowhere to be seen, and I had no idea of how to contact him.

Lighting up a cigarette, I sat down to think, and after calming down, my mind started to work. I vaguely remembered someone telling me about the shuttle bus system American airports run. Sure enough, when I asked at information, I was directed to where I could catch one to Fort Lauderdale. In my rush to get out of Miami Airport, I forgot to change some of my precious pounds to dollars and didn't realise this until I jumped on the bus. Explaining that someone would be paying my fare at the other end was thankfully not a problem. I just hoped and prayed that this would be the case. It was with such great relief that I saw Roy standing at the entrance to Bahia Mar Marina when the bus pulled up. Once I got off the bus and he paid the fare I just burst into tears, and it took a lot of hugging before I managed to pull myself together. Bob had offered to drive Roy to the airport, and after they had waited a long time and were then told all passengers from my flight had already come through, Bob convinced Roy that I must have missed the flight, and they drove back to Fort Lauderdale. Once back at the marina Roy thought about it and decided that no way would I have missed the flight. I just would not have done that. He then guessed that for some reason I had been held up at the airport and was hoping I would figure out catching a shuttle bus. He therefore decided his best option was to wait at the entrance, hoping he was correct in his assumption. Thank God he did. Bahia Mar Marina was vast, containing hundreds of boats, and I would have had a real problem finding Atlast quickly whilst the bus driver waited to be paid, with a bunch of passengers not happy with the delay. I will always hate Miami Airport.

Chapter 14 – Intrepid Dragon II

Once my case was dumped on board, Roy and I went over to the marina café for a late lunch. Bob and Ruby had already gone off somewhere for theirs. We did laugh over the way we managed to get Atlast into the ship, and Roy was highly amused when I told him about the anchor dropping. Apparently, when he came to, the first thing he was aware of was engine noise, but he was confused as he knew Atlast wasn't on the move. Reading my hurried note made things a lot clearer. After making himself known to the ship's crew, he was given a cabin for the rest of the voyage. He kept himself busy by making use of his sextant, mostly taking noon sights, and was delighted to find that when he compared his position to the ship's instrument results their positions were very close. I never did ask him how he managed to manoeuvre the boat into the marina singlehanded. I expect the marina staff assisted. Ever since arriving, Roy spent many hours removing a black greasy substance on both the outside and inside of the boat. The horrible stuff managed to get into every nook and cranny, and even into some of the cupboards. So much for doing all that cleaning beforehand.

When we got back to the boat Bob and Ruby were waiting for us. They had decided it would be a good idea if Ruby took me to the local supermarket so that I could buy enough food to feed Roy and myself for the next ten days or so before they returned. Great, thought I. By then I was well into feeling jet-lagged and all I wanted to do was to have a kip. I was allowed to have a quick shower and change of clothes before I was whisked off. I had grabbed my notebook, and whilst Ruby was driving, I struggled trying to make a list of all the things we would need. Shopping with Ruby was quite an ordeal as she kept questioning everything I picked up, often suggesting alternatives. She was a bit of a health freak and was truly doing my head in. I rapidly came to the conclusion that she and I were never going to be bosom friends. I was so relieved once we returned to the boat, put all the food away and said goodbye to Bob and Ruby. At long last Roy and I were on our own.

We fell into a 'boat in marina' routine with our daily work, just like everyone else around us. Every morning boats were hosed down and wiped, with everywhere below deck kept spotless. After lunch you would hear quite a few engines being run, sometimes ours as well, and often tenders were given a little run to make sure the outboards worked. By day four I was getting bored and would often wander off for a while, taking in that part of Fort Lauderdale. I soon discovered that most of the large powerboats used Bahia Mar Marina, whereas Pier 66 Marina across the way tended to be favoured by the sailing world. Judging by the cost of their sandwiches, I reckon Bahia Mar was a lot more expensive. Naturally Roy and I tended to do our socialising at Pier 66, where we met up with quite a few friends of friends and were therefore able to keep up to date with some of the sailing gossip. How I missed not being on a sailing boat and that whole friendly environment.

On Bob and Ruby's next visit I was given a bag containing some clothes. Ruby said she hoped she had got the sizes correct, but it was not a problem if they needed changing. Roy and I both looked askance at Bob, who sheepishly informed us that they were our uniforms. This had never been discussed beforehand, and I think both our faces told it all. Bob then hastily explained that they were only for us to wear when we had guests on board. Beige trousers and white shirts – yuk! Roy even had a hat with gold trim. With his naval background, I knew there was no way he would ever wear it. I had this awful vision of being subservient to a lot of demanding people. This was definitely not what I had signed up for. I wanted out, big time. The only good thing that came out of this was that Ruby took us to a shoe shop to be fitted out with expensive Docksiders. Those I would keep.

Once they left, both Roy and I agreed that we really must find another job, and quick. He had already got to know one boat agent, Frank Atlas, who seemed to be well in the know, so off he went to have a chat with him. In the meantime I went to visit neighbours Ruth and Ben Travers who were crew on a slightly smaller but much prettier powerboat. On our first meeting with them we immediately got on together like a house on fire. They had a small apartment close by and very kindly invited us to spend Christmas with them, which was fast approaching. They found it quite amusing that we were so unhappy with the uniforms. It was the norm for the powerboat fraternity and all part of the job. They were a lovely couple. For Ruth it was her third marriage. Ben was all action, but Ruth, who came from the south, was a lot more laid-back. She produced the most amazing Christmas lunch. We had turkey with slick dumplings, a southern dish of thin pieces of dough cooked in the juice of the meat, with all sorts of vegetables and pineapple pie as a savoury. It was so incredibly tasty. In return we invited them onto our boat for New Year's Eve, when I cooked a typical English roast which went down well.

So here we were in 1975. Two weeks into the New Year Bob paid us a visit, this time on his own. I could tell something was up as he didn't look too happy. He started to ask Roy what he had been doing with his time during working hours. This took us both by surprise as we had genuinely been very fair with him, and the boat was always in tip-top condition with everything in good working order. Bob then asked Roy if he had been checking the level of oil in the engines, and wanted to be shown. All very odd. I could hear raised voices coming from the engine room including Roy's, which I had never heard before. What on earth was going on? Roy came back into the saloon with a face like thunder and said to me, 'Pack our bags. We are leaving right now.'

I looked at Bob, but all he said was, 'Sorry.' Half an hour later we were on the dock with our bags, with Bob paying Roy what was owed to us. We then grabbed a taxi and headed off to Frank Atlas's office. En route we came to the conclusion that Bob must have found out about Roy being too drunk to drive Atlast into the hull of the merchant ship back in Cowes. We reckoned he got to know this through the owner of the sister boat Laurie Nan, who was a friend of his, and guessed it originally came from the skipper, Kev. It would be just the sort of thing he would have done. We could just imagine him and the owner of Laurie Nan having a good laugh over it all, but of course Bob would certainly not have seen the funny side. Hey ho – it was his loss really as he actually did lose a damn good skipper. As it turned out, Kev had done us a big favour by spilling the beans.

Frank was great. He reckoned he had one or two things in the pipeline for us, but in the meantime he suggested we stayed on Athena, a lovely old 70 ft ketch moored at the bottom of his garden. It belonged to a friend of his and was on his books for selling. We earnt our keep by cleaning up the yacht, and Roy made sure it was kept in good working order. We also took it out on a short sailing trip as Frank wanted to make sure all the sailing tackle was working and that there were no split seams in the sails. All was good, which was surprising for quite an old boat, and she sailed really well. I also managed to earn a little extra money by doing a one-week charter on Che Che, who needed a cook/hostess. It was skippered by an old friend of Roy's, Andy Ackerman. Just a few weeks later Frank came down to see us with a big smile on his face. Someone who had just bought one of his boats was looking for a skipper and mate to look after it. He thought it would really suit us and that the owner would like us very much. He was half laughing whilst telling us this so we became very wary. The owner wanted 'red sails in the sunset', so what Frank came up with was an 80 ft Chinese Junk weighing 100 tons which came complete with red sails and gold dragons. It was love at first sight. It also came out in conversation that he loved the British, and therefore Frank felt we would be perfect for this new boat owner. He then showed us a brochure of the boat. Intrepid Dragon II was its name, and 'wow' was the only word I could come up with. It had a lot of varnished wood and brass work, and an amazing amount of Chinese carving below decks. It was built in Hong Kong in 1969 for an American chap who then sailed it back to Florida. At present it was in West Palm Beach having some work done as part of the sale agreement.

It was arranged for us to meet the owner, Jules Nelson, at the boatyard in four days' time. Both the owner and the boat were unique. Jules had a bushy moustache and dark curly hair, laughing eyes and a face that looked like it could tell a million stories. If you put a Mexican hat and poncho on him and stuck a cigar in his mouth, he would look like a genuine bandito. When I mentioned this to him some time later he declared that he had made his first lot of money gunrunning to Cuba. I assumed he was teasing ... or was he?

This time we were not disappointed with the boat. It was

even more impressive in real life. On each side of the bow was an enormous thirty-foot gold painted dragon mounted on a board that extended to at least ten feet beyond the bow. It was ketch rigged with all three red sails being fully bamboo battened, and surprisingly the rigging was solid stainless steel. There was also an additional small sail forward of the jib which we ended up calling the 'baby sail'. Below deck was truly amazing. There were beautiful teak carvings in the saloon and the huge master bedroom which had an American queen-size bed and en-suite shower room. Both rooms had deep red carpeting. On the aft wall of the saloon four Chinese screens were mounted, depicting each of the four seasons through pieces of jade mounted on black lacquered boards. Forward of the galley was a cabin with twin bunks and another shower room. A lot of boat for accommodating just four people. The engine room with its 300 hp Cummins engine was also huge, with plenty of headroom and shelving for food and spares storage, along with a very large water tank and four fuel tanks. Not only was there an additional storage area in the lazarette at the stern of the boat, but it also had a bunk and toilet for a crew member. I also spotted a couple of decent fishing rods and two Raleigh fold-up bicycles, which really delighted me. It was a lot to take in and left us both rather speechless. This boat was most certainly one of a kind.

We instantly got on with Jules and could tell he was very pleased with us. He had a great sense of humour. Both his adopted sons and his niece were all at boarding school in England as he strongly believed in our educational system, and he made it quite clear that he loved anything British and tried to spend as much time as possible in England. It was estimated that the work on the hull would take eight weeks, so it was agreed that we would start our job in four weeks' time. This would allow us to familiarise ourselves with the boat and start the clean-up and provisioning as preparation for taking her to Philadelphia, which was where Jules lived. We would do this mostly via the Intracoastal Waterway which runs for 3,000 miles from Boston in Massachusetts in the north, along the east coast of the Atlantic, all the way down to the tip of Florida and round into the Gulf of Mexico, up to Texas. The natural lakes and inlets were linked by a number of man-made canals which included Cape Cod, Chesapeake and Delaware, and the Dismal Swamp. It was originally built so that commercial traffic could avoid the hazards of the open sea and is now made full use of by pleasure boats.

One of the major things that needed doing was fixing the propeller. At some stage in the past it must have had a severe hammering as it was badly bent and battered. A place in Jacksonville confirmed that they could repair it almost straight away and that the work would take two days to complete. Once we joined the boat, the next thing I knew I was heading north on Interstate Route 95 driving a car that was big enough for the prop to fit in the boot. Back then, due to fuel shortage, the maximum speed limit was 55 mph. It didn't take long before I become frustrated keeping to that speed as I love driving fast. I remembered that if you follow a truck that is speeding, you knew they had a ham radio set and were being told where the 'smokies' (speed patrol police) were hiding or on the move up ahead. Most commercial vehicles and a lot of private cars had them for this very purpose. It wasn't long before I latched onto a truck and found myself happily doing 70+ mph. When he slowed down, so did I, and sure enough there would be a police car either hiding behind a bush or by one of the bridge piers. Not far from Jacksonville the truck turned off, giving me a big wave. I stupidly forgot to ease off the gas pedal, and before I knew it, I was being flashed down to pull over. Damn! One of the two policemen sauntered over and asked me to step out of the car. Boy, was I nervous, especially seeing his hand wavering above his gun in his holster. I shakily got out and followed him to the patrol car where I was asked to sit in the rear passenger seat. I was then informed that I had been clocked driving 94 mph, which genuinely surprised me. Having already given him my international driving licence, I was asked where I came from. I said in my sweetest voice, 'England,' and explained that the speeds were a lot higher there, and even more so in France where I had been used to driving, which was a lie. I then apologised and said, 'These lovely large American cars are so smooth and quiet, you just don't realise how fast you are driving.' I got a heavy lecture but was let off as they hated to book foreigners. Phew!

After dropping off the prop, I found a Travelodge to wait out the time in until the job was completed. I have to say I didn't feel too comfortable being on my own in that sort of environment. I spent most of the time in my room and would take a book to read when I sat at my solitary table at meal times. On the second evening I plucked up enough courage to order a nightcap at the bar, and ended up having a chat with a couple of travelling salesmen. They were most pleasant and kindly gave me an easier route back to the I-95 south, avoiding the city traffic. The following morning I picked up the vastly improved prop and successfully followed the directions given to me. Once I reached the I-95 I hit the gas pedal and headed towards a truck I could see in the distance. I could not believe it when once again there were flashing lights behind me. The same routine happened and I repeated my excuses. Just as one of the policemen started the expected lecture, a voice came over the radio and said, 'Is that Teresa Pegg with an international driving licence? I stopped her going north two days ago'.

The policeman's eyebrows went up and my head went down as I muttered, 'Shit.'

'Well, young lady, you certainly have not learnt your lesson. Doing 88 mph means we should be taking you down to the jailhouse, but we don't want to do that. Instead, I am going to say you were doing 79 mph, which will cost you a hundred bucks.' Fortunately I had sufficient cash on me to pay this instant fine.

A little later than expected, we finally left West Palm Beach on Wednesday 2 July. We had an additional crew member, Ward, who was a student from Cornwall back in England. He was taking a gap year and had decided to hitch-hike to Cowes on the Isle of Wight. He ended up crewing a yacht across the Atlantic, and apparently his parents only learnt about this upon his arrival in Antigua. He managed to work his way up to Fort Lauderdale, which was where we met him. We really needed an extra pair of hands on board, and he readily agreed to join us. Roy immediately put him to work cleaning out the engine room and lazarette.

Due to the weight of the boat we knew we would be motoring a lot. It was really a motorsailer, and we now understood why there was plenty of fuel storage. Our first destination was Morehead City in North Carolina. With Intrepid's eight-foot draft we decided to go along the coast rather than risk being grounded travelling along that part of the Intracoastal, which was known to be quite shallow. To begin with we experienced some rough seas, so it wasn't until the second day that we were able to put up all the sails. Boy, were they heavy, especially the main. It took both Ward and I our full strength to get it up. Going about was a real dockyard job. Each batten had a guide rope, so we had to come up into wind and hold the boat there whilst one of us whipped all the guide ropes to the other side. No way could this be done quickly. Once we did get all the sails up and turn the engine off, it was quite impressive to see this heavy monster of a boat glide through the waves under sail.

Sadly, it was short-lived as we needed at least three knots of wind to get her moving, and it wasn't long before it dropped to just two knots. Most of the time we ended up motorsailing with just the mainsail up.

We soon discovered that poor Intrepid had not been properly maintained for some time. This meant that Roy was constantly kept busy fixing something or other, leaving Ward and I to do most of the steering. Due to a leaky porthole, the engine room had to be regularly pumped out as soon as there were any signs of waves. In the four days it took to reach Morehead City, Roy had to regularly top up the main engine with water due to a leak, the fuel pump had to be cleaned out, some of the bamboo battens were temporarily strapped due to splits, and the mizzen shroud broke. The defects list was getting longer by the minute. Thank goodness Roy was very much a DIY type of guy and was an electrician by trade. Jules was definitely getting full value for money as far as Roy was concerned. We spent one day in the Morehead City Yacht Basin doing as much repair work as we possibly could before carrying on. Shortly after leaving Morehead City we joined the Intracoastal, which made for more gentle sailing. Each day we put in about twelve hours before dropping anchor or mooring at a marina for the night. When we arrived at Solomon's Island we had a rest day and then yet another day fixing things. This time it was the 1.5 hp backup outboard for the tender, which we reckoned hadn't been working for a long time, and the battery charger, which had ceased working. What next?

No sooner had we started off again, the raw water pump stopped working. Roy was a keen amateur radio operator and had a ham radio set installed on Intrepid. If you were able to connect with another amateur operator local to someone you wanted to contact, they would be able to link you to that person by landline. Thanks to satellite communication, these days this is old hat, but it was very good news back then, especially if you were able to pick up a good signal in the middle of the ocean. Through the radio, Roy managed to make contact with Jules and ask him to get replacement parts to us in Annapolis, where we managed to limp into later that day. It took a week for the parts to arrive. In the meantime we did a lot of varnishing on deck, and Roy finally got the saloon air conditioning working. After clearing the radar visor, he discovered three new bulbs were needed; yet another task for the ever-increasing list.

With great relief, and much to Jules's delight, we finally arrived in Philadelphia on 24 July. We said goodbye to Ward soon after as he had to get back to UK to start his degree the following month. It was a pleasure having him on board, and I often wonder how he fared. For someone who at first thought he would only get to the Isle of Wight before returning home, he achieved a far greater adventure, and I hope it pointed him in the right direction for doing well in life. Once I had cleaned the boat from top to bottom, I decided to try out one of the collapsible bikes and explore this wonderful historical city. Roy was never one for sightseeing and was quite content to carry on fixing things on the boat. I was surprised but delighted to see cobbled streets and a working tram, and once I managed to obtain a map of the city I headed straight to Independence Hall. I thoroughly enjoyed my day and loved the older parts of the city that I saw, realising once again how much I preferred exploring old buildings and narrow streets.

Chapter 15 – The Intracoastal

Roy and I realised that our maximum stay in America was about to expire, so we did a very quick trip to Toronto, staying with Joyce and Bill Hawksby who were very old friends of my parents. In fact, Joyce and my mum used to go to school together. With their three children Joyce and Bill took advantage of the government incentive of £5 a ticket to emigrate to either Canada, Australia or New Zealand, and they chose Canada. I was about four when they left, and I still have the teddy bear that their eldest son Graham gave me. Mum and Dad were seriously thinking of doing the same, but to New Zealand, and even had all the paperwork ready to complete. They were about to go ahead when my grandad tragically died in an accident. Mum couldn't leave her own mum at that time, so we never did emigrate. As it turned out, my sister Janet's second marriage was to a Kiwi farmer, and she has lived in New Zealand for the past forty-odd years, resulting in Mum and Dad visiting them a number of times.

Bill and Joyce looked after us extremely well during the three days we spent with them, and we got to see Niagara Falls which was not far from where they lived. We did leave a message for Jules to let him know where we were, but whether he didn't get the message or forgot, he was not best pleased to find we were not on board on one of his regular visits to the boat. I believe he must have had some friends with him. A few days after our return we were woken up at around 0200 with people jumping on board. It was Jules with the Four Tops in tow. They had been partying together after one of the band's concerts and decided to have a nightcap on the boat. Roy and I hastily got dressed, and with bleary eyes, served up some drinks and snacks. Jules had a very mischievous grin on his face and said that it served us right for not being there the last time he visited.

It was summer school holiday time so the kids were back from England, and we were asked if we would take them on a week's cruise up to New York. Jeff was sixteen at the time, Mimi was fifteen and Bryan was around ten. Used to doing sail training in the navy, this was no problem for Roy, and in fact he was looking forward to having them on board. I was a little apprehensive as having a kid sister in their age group, I had a little knowledge that dealing with teenagers could often be challenging; plus it wasn't that long ago that I was one myself. They joined us on 11 August, and by late afternoon we were on our way. Being used to boarding school, the kids settled in very quickly and were genuinely interested in sailing. What really helped was that Roy treated them just like the young cadets he used to teach, and being so laid-back in giving them plenty of responsibility meant they were keen to show us they were adult enough to handle it. We made sure they were kept busy all the time to avoid that dreaded word 'boring' being uttered.

The first night we anchored in the Chesapeake and Delaware Canal. During supper Roy drew up a watch system for himself and the kids in true naval fashion which set the tone and allowed each person to steer for an hour a time. First watch was to start at 0600 the following morning. Surprisingly, there were no complaints, and even more surprisingly, they were ready on time. Roy took the first watch whilst I briefed them on how to use the windlass to bring up the anchor. Next stop Atlantic City. It was a choppy day but the kids coped well and no one was seasick. All meals including supper were eaten underway. At 2200 hours we finally managed to obtain a berth at one of the marinas. Being quite shallow we touched the bottom, so we only just managed to get alongside by pulling hard on the mooring ropes. We had a late start the following morning as once again we were delayed whilst Roy had to do some repair work – this time it was refixing the raw water pipe to the starboard exhaust. Thanks to better weather conditions the kids got their first experience of putting up the sails. Under Roy's direction he left them to do all the work and they really enjoyed it, and we could see how chuffed they were to see the results of all their hard work. Intrepid was sailing at a good speed without her engine. All went well until a squall hit us in the late afternoon. Having very little warning, it was all hands on deck to get the sails down in a hurry before we were hit with winds of forty knots just before we got into port, and this continued as we were berthing at the Bimini Yacht Club which was quite a challenge with an inexperienced crew. Unfortunately, we ended up losing one of the dragon's feet in the process of docking.

There was great excitement the following morning as we were going to be sailing up the Hudson River through New York. Once again the kids were able to get all the sails up and were able to keep them up whilst taking in the sights of New York. As you can imagine, Intrepid caused a great deal of interest from both those on the river and along the shore. With all the sails up she really was very impressive. We couldn't get into the marina at Gravesend Bay in Brooklyn, and although we tried there wasn't anywhere suitable along the bank, so we had to anchor off which was a shame. By 0930 the following day we continued up the Hudson – this time under engine – passing very close to the Statue of Liberty, and managed to get a berth in the World Fair Marina in Flushing, in the neighbourhood of Queens, in good time for the kids to explore ashore before supper and again the following morning. We left after lunch and motored around to Yacht Haven East in Stamford, Connecticut, for the kids' final night on board. They really did have a great time, and we thoroughly enjoyed their company. They were being picked up after breakfast the next day. We said our farewells and they hoped they would meet us again when they returned for their Christmas break. Roy and I spent the rest of the day clearing up, and had a well-earned, relaxing evening with just the two of us.

Jules asked us to continue on to Newport, Rhode Island, as he wanted to spend a few days there, which really delighted us. We were so close it would have been a pity not to get to see the place. It is one of the major international meeting places for 'grotty yachties' – Cowes, Antigua and Fort Lauderdale being the other main ones. So, on Monday 18 August, the day after the kids left, we carried on to Newport RI, arriving there the following day. We were fortunate to be able to dock alongside the old Bannisters Wharf which is right in the middle of the lovely old part of the town. Amusingly parked on the wharf close by was a red double-decker London Bus. Being right in the heart of this historic part of Newport did have a couple of disadvantages. One day whilst below decks we heard someone jump on board. Normally if there is a visitor, the polite thing to do is to call out and wait for permission to board. I rushed up on deck and was confronted with a stranger.

'Can I help?' said I.

'Nope,' said he, 'I'm just having a look around.'

In a very indignant voice, using my best attempt at a posh English accent, I said, 'Excuse me, this is my home. Would you like it if I just walked in the front door of your house and said the same thing?' He was most put out and reluctantly climbed back up the ladder to the wharf. How rude!

There was always a crowd of people looking down from the dock, so the curtains were often kept closed for privacy. Another time, I was working on deck when I suddenly felt something fall by the side of me. Someone above had thrown me a sweet! It took all of my control not to act like a monkey and go jumping around the deck.

We had such a lovely, sociable time there meeting so many new boatie people and also some of the elite locals. A reporter interviewed us, and once the article was printed in the local rag we became famous and popular as the 'novel' guests at a few cocktail parties. Our best casual clothes did not come close to being suitable attire amongst the silks and cravats. As we entered each of these magnificent and very opulent houses, I had a hard job keeping my jaw closed and acting as if this was quite a normal environment for me. I reckon each host was trying to outdo their neighbours with the canapés – they were out of this world, and I tried hard not to make it obvious how many I was scoffing.

I loved exploring ashore. I learnt that quite of few of the old colonial buildings did not originally belong there. They were literally picked up from other places and moved there, and carefully restored back to their original state. Layers of paint were painstakingly removed until the original layer was reached, and then that colour was matched for repainting. On one of my excursions, this time with Roy in tow, I noticed there was a big sign up at the flower shop saying 'Kittens for free'. I think there were four or five, but the one that caught my eye was a grey and white one clinging to a parakeet cage with one very unhappy bird squawking inside. It was instant love for this kitten. I asked the flower girl if I could have it, and when she said I could, I picked it up and headed straight back to the boat, with Roy following behind saying we couldn't possibly have a cat on board. I totally ignored all his protests until he finally gave in. I think the kitten was part Burmese. He was mostly smoky grey but had a white nose with four white paws, so Boots became his name.

Jules was arriving the following day and I hoped like crazy he would not object or even be allergic to cats. I need not have worried. He took one look at me cuddling the kitten with a pleading look on my face and burst out laughing. Our new crew member was accepted. Jules only stayed for a few days to see some friends and then left. I was lucky enough to enjoy my birthday on 19 September in this lovely place, celebrating with lots of new friends. We finally and reluctantly left on 24 September, spending one day in Essex, Connecticut, (I had to see another Essex!) before turning back. It was there that Roy was excited to discover mushrooms growing in the grass at the marina. When he showed them to other boatie people, including our friend Fran who had popped over to see us, they were all sceptical and said no way would they risk eating them. As he was adamant that he wanted the mushrooms for breakfast, I cooked them up, and although I too thought they were safe I have to admit I was greatly relieved that neither of us suffered any bad after-effects. Whilst there, we made friends with Mike McMillan who was on another boat but looking for a lift back to Brooklyn, where he lived. As soon as he saw Boots, he recognised the kitten. It was one of his own cat's litter. He had brought them to the flower girl, who was a friend, and asked her to give them away free to good homes. He was delighted that we had one of them and made a big fuss of him. Boots was seasick on his first day on board, but after that he soon became a seasoned boat cat, and he and I became inseparable. If he got impatient whilst I was preparing his food, he would nip my ankle – he always knew which one was the real one. In return, I would pick him up and bite his tail. We understood each other well. He fell overboard on his second day but managed to get out and back on board by himself. One soggy moggy. He learnt a lesson, and as he was born in Brooklyn, I had a feeling Boots would be a survivor. This he certainly proved to be. More about his escapades later!

On 27 September we turned around and headed south, and had lunch in Manhattan before saying goodbye to Mike. Our destination was Fort Lauderdale, where Jules wanted to base the boat for a while, which put a big smile on both our faces. Two days later, back in the Chesapeake and Delaware Canal we met up with a couple who told us they knew the boat from a year or so back when it was used to make a pornographic film. That caught Roy's interest. Just as well we didn't have Google or any other online search engine back then. They also told us that whilst the boat was previously in the US Virgin Islands, the skipper was arrested for carrying drugs. This was a concern as there were so many places on the boat where a stash could be hidden. I had a good look, but I found it virtually impossible to do a really thorough search as there were a lot of double layers of linings due to all the wood carvings.

Once again Boots fell overboard just as we were about to leave the following morning. This time he was rescued by some workmen, which was just as well as we hadn't noticed him go. We arrived in Annapolis at the end of September and remained there for three weeks catching up on general maintenance and small repairs. Intrepid was gradually becoming a great deal more shipshape, and with lots of new varnish and polished brass work she really was looking more like her old original self.

Annapolis was yet another place I loved. The capital of Maryland, it sits on the edge of beautiful Chesapeake Bay. It is full of naval history and has many old brick buildings dating back to the eighteenth century, along with the amazing earlier-built State House. It had a very colonial feel, and I loved the many stylish shops and restaurants dotted along the harbour frontage. Once again I was in my element treading ancient steps, exploring lots of old nooks and crannies. I also loved being in such a large centre for boating, and hearing the tinkling of halyards tapping against the masts was, and still is, music to my ears. I learnt that the Chesapeake Bay area is famous for its seafood, particularly crab and oysters which are often served minced up and made into delicious fishcakes. It was here that I first experienced eating soft-shell crabs, which were amazingly good. We got to meet many interesting and fun-loving people including Ernie, who was a chef at our favourite fish restaurant. One evening Ernie cooked us an incredible meal on board and brought some of his special sauce. No amount of alcohol managed to persuade him to let me have that recipe.

When we set off on 20 October we discovered the generator battery was flat, so Roy had to jump-start it from the main engine supply. I swear that boat mischievously waited until we were back at sea before making something else not work. Then, surprise, surprise, on the following day in Great Bridge, Virginia, we caught up with Laurie Nan, the sister ship of Atlast. I made sure the skipper, Kev, knew we had guessed who had spilled the beans back in Cowes, and enjoyed making him feel sheepish and somewhat uncomfortable about it. It was good to see Marg again and we made them both welcome on board, and of course they were impressed with Intrepid, which was my intention. Up yours, Kev! Virtually straight after bumping into Laurie Nan we caught up with a yacht, Tivoli, and who should be on board? None other than our dear friend Mike Whitaker, last seen taking Atlast into the ship back in Cowes. What an amazing coincidence. It certainly is a small world, especially when it comes to moving around on boats. Mike was on a delivery down to Miami. It was great to catch up with him, and we had quite a chuckle reminiscing over what happened in Cowes.

We slowly made our way through North and South Carolina, meeting lots of interesting people along the way. I was, however, shocked to discover that there was still quite a lot of prejudice in this part of the south, which left me wanting to end a conversation quickly on more than one occasion. I thoroughly enjoyed the wonderful experience of seeing so much wildlife, including pods of dolphins and many birds, and unsurprisingly we spotted the occasional alligator. Every day we would put out the two fishing rods at the stern and if we were lucky, we would catch a fish for supper. Boots soon knew what the sound of the wire whizzing through the reel meant. This time, Roy decided to risk staying in the Intracoastal through Florida due to poor weather conditions forecasted along the coast. The first time we went aground was in Rattlesnake Cut in Daytona, but we managed to get going again fairly quickly. From then onwards it was slow-going as we bottomed quite a few times, and at one stage we were stuck for two hours. They were long days, and we often had to wait for a number of bridges to open. Most mornings we were away by 0600 and either alongside or at anchor by 1900. If we managed to get alongside somewhere, Boots would immediately jump ashore and explore. Often there would be someone fishing off the end of the pier and Boots would cunningly sit beside the person, looking into the bucket of small fish bait. Sure enough, he would return to the boat with a fish in his mouth. He was certainly learning to survive. When we were ready to leave, as soon as we called him he would come immediately. No way was he going to be left behind.

Fixing things, or if unable to do so, adding it to the defects list, was part of Roy's daily routine. Eventually the list was long enough to warrant a boatyard visit. After discussing things with Jules we booked into Lantana Boatyard, arriving there on 15 November. We were hauled out, as a number of things had to be done to the hull. Whilst waiting for this to happen I made full use of the launderette on the fuel dock. On one of my trips back and forth I slipped getting off the boat, and nearly fell in between the boat and the dock. A lady came to my aid and managed to help me back onto dry land. When she asked me if I was all right, looking down at my artificial leg, I realised the foot was dangling. My reply was therefore quite casual: 'Oh, it's okay, it's just the ankle joint that has broken.' She immediately went into panic, thinking I would need an ambulance. When I explained the situation we had a good laugh, and she said she would never forget me. It was a good job I had a spare leg, as the bolt holding the leg to the rocker joint of the ankle had sheared off. I managed to make a phone call to Roehampton, and dear Dr Fletcher said that he would send some spare ankle parts to Fort Lauderdale straight away. I doubt very much if you would get that kind of service on the NHS nowadays.

It was rather scary being up so high once the boat was out of water, and climbing up and down the tall ladder was not easy for me. I had to look down to make sure my wooden foot was firmly on the next step before proceeding down. I was amazed to see that Boots managed it, going sideways down on each step. It was a real pain living on board during this time as we couldn't use the loo on the boat. I shall never forget the shower block in that boatyard. Just inside the entrance to the toilets there was a large bin for the wet paper towels. Cockroaches lived in it and they were disgustingly huge. Whilst sitting on the toilet I could hear rustling as they moved about, and one time I saw these large antennae appear under the door, heading towards me. With my knickers and shorts only halfway up, I flew out of the cubicle. It is the one and only bug I absolutely loathe. From then onwards I made sure I always carried a can of Baygon with me to kill the buggers. After eleven more days we finally left the boatyard and arrived in Fort Lauderdale eight hours later. There was no room for us in Bahia Mar so we ended up in Le Club International. It was so lovely to be back in Fort Lauderdale, and as soon as possible we headed over to Pier 66 Marina to catch up with old friends and pick up the latest yachtie gossip, all done over a number of jugs of beer.

One of the things that desperately needed sorting on Intrepid was the replacement of some of the bamboo battens, particularly two of the larger ones on the mainsail. After an exhaustive search Roy was unable to find a supplier who could provide any bamboo large and thick enough. A local chap told Roy where he knew there was some, and off they went to see. It was in a private estate, and there, close to the boundary fence, was a very large clump of bamboo, some of it certainly large enough. So one night, Roy, with three others, sneaked over there with a couple of saws to cut some down. I was so nervous they would get caught and was therefore greatly relieved when Roy returned with a big smile, saying, 'Mission accomplished.' Phew! I had visions of them being shot at by one nervous owner, or even by his security guards.

Jules decided that it would be a great idea for all the family to spend Christmas on the boat at Paradise Island, Nassau, in the Bahamas. Although he was Jewish, he celebrated the event as the kids hadn't been brought up in the same faith. He also discussed the possibility of us taking the boat over to Europe. He rather fancied the Greek Islands. Roy and I were delighted at the prospect and confirmed that it was feasible. I couldn't have been happier, and was excited about all that was ahead of us. My mind was full of food ideas, and I was determined to provide a traditional English Christmas lunch complete with turkey, roast potatoes and all the trimmings, and of course

Christmas pudding and cake. I was loving life.

We left Fort Lauderdale at the beginning of December and headed back to Lantana Boatyard. The small electric fridge/freezer on board was small and often didn't work properly. It was therefore decided to replace it with separate gas units for both fridge and freezer installed side by side. This involved reorganising the galley cupboards and extending the gas pipework round from the cooker. Unfortunately, the delivery of the fridges was delayed and they arrived just in time to be installed the day before we were due to leave for the Bahamas. The saloon was piled high with the contents of the cupboards plus bags and bags of extra provisions I had bought in readiness for the trip. I also made full use of the excellent supermarkets in Fort Lauderdale by stocking up on everything needed for the catering I would be doing over the Christmas period. This included quite a few English imports that were essential for my intended Christmas spread, leaving just fresh food to buy in the market at Nassau. In amongst all this chaos, Tom, a friend of Jules, joined us as a welcome additional crew member. The guys at the boatyard did a good job in getting the fridges installed and working, and reassembled the altered cupboards in double quick time. Thankfully by the evening we had everything stored away before we headed ashore for some well-earned cold beers and supper.

A few days before leaving for Nassau I borrowed Tom's hire car to whizz back to Fort Lauderdale to collect some mail that had arrived at Frank Atlas' office, which he kindly allowed us to use as our mailing address whilst in Florida. I didn't get far before I ended up having an accident. I was following a motorcyclist, and just after a junction he suddenly stopped dead right in front of me. Apparently, his chain broke and wrapped itself round the rear wheel. To my horror I hit the bike, sending the guy flying through the air and hitting my windscreen before bouncing off onto the road. I was quite amazed at how quickly the emergency vehicles arrived. Someone must have had a car phone. State patrol and local police cars, an ambulance and even a fire engine came upon the scene from various directions almost instantly. By this time I was kneeling by the side of the injured young chap, trying to stop him thrashing about wildly whilst shouting to God that he was hurting. At least he was making noise. The good news was that more than one person gave their name as a witness, stating that there was no way I could have avoided hitting him. One of the policemen took my statement, and after giving him my current address I was allowed to go. As I was badly shaken up and the windscreen was cracked, I turned around and headed back to the boat. One look at my face told Roy all was not well.

The following day the police turned up to complete the paperwork. Apparently the guy had no tax or insurance, and they wanted me to say he was driving dangerously. They really wanted to throw the book at him. I made it quite clear that that was not the case. I had followed him for some time without a problem. It was just bad luck that the chain broke when it did. I wanted to go and see the guy in hospital to make sure he was okay, but was firmly advised by Tom that no way should I get more involved. He was wise. On Jules's next visit he brought a letter addressed to me. It was from an attorney informing me that I, along with the car hire company and Tom as the hirer, were all being sued on behalf of the injured person. When I showed the letter to Jules, he laughed, tore it up and said to forget it. All quite normal for the US of A. Arrgh!

Chapter 16 – Serious Dragon Sailing

We left after breakfast on 10 December and headed north to Palm Beach for our final night in the Intracoastal before heading out to sea the following morning. Two days later, due to bad weather we motored into the Berry Islands for shelter, where we were stuck for three days, waiting for the wind to die down and hopefully change course. I made full use of this time by making both the Christmas pudding and the Christmas cake, creating tantalising smells which were a real tease for us all. It was beginning to feel like Christmas. We managed to get to Bird Island where we sheltered once again for the night before finally arriving at Paradise Island marina the following morning with winds still blowing at forty knots. It was a relief to be safely tied up alongside in our reserved berth. Looking around, even with the sun hiding behind big ugly clouds and a grey choppy sea, it was obvious we were in a very pretty place. The marina was between two hotels: the Atlantis, which had a casino, and the Britannia. When I woke up in the morning and went up on deck, I wasn't disappointed. The sun was shining and the now calm sea was glistening, with spectacular colours ranging from the lightest pale blue to the deeper blues beyond. The water was extremely clear and I was fascinated watching so many different brightly coloured fish swimming around the boat. Boots was already ashore exploring.

We only had one day to sort things out before Jules and his wife, Claire, her brother Ron, Ron's oldest son, Stacey, and the three kids back from school descended upon us. By this time Tom had already left us to be back home for the holidays. It was a squeeze but we managed to sleep everyone below decks, with Roy and I happily snuggled down on the spacious aft deck under the awning. The following day we sailed over to Ship Channel Cay, a small private island in the Exumas. Thanks to the improved weather conditions we managed to hoist the sails which was such a treat, and of course the kids were delighted to show off their sailing knowledge to their parents. After dropping the anchor we all went ashore in the dory to explore. The Exumas were used as a location for the early James Bond film Thunderball. As I stood on the soft white sandy beach looking out at the many shades of blue water, the scene of Ursula Andress walking out of the sea in that amazing bikini singing 'The Mango Tree' in the film Dr No came vividly to mind. I was fourteen when I saw the film and thought it was the most glamorous thing ever, with scenes so beautiful and exotic. Although it wasn't filmed in the Bahamas, I couldn't believe here I was thirteen years later, standing somewhere just as amazing. It really was such a far-removed thought for me, as a young Essex girl, to believe that one day I would be in such a place that I only expected to see in expensive glossy holiday brochures, and far beyond my reach financially. I remember feeling overwhelmed with these thoughts and thinking what a very lucky and fortunate girl I was.

The following day we went across to Highborne Cay to check out the marina, which Jules particularly wanted to do. We were back in Paradise Island on 21 December and it was all go getting ready for Christmas. On the corner table in the saloon I put up a small artificial Christmas tree complete with baubles that I bought in Fort Lauderdale, and then started on the food preparations, doing as much as I could in advance. This included baking a batch of mince pies, making the turkey stuffing and bread sauce, and icing the Christmas cake. I love local markets, and Nassau did not disappoint. It was huge and buzzing with lots of people laughing and shouting to each other. It was just like being back in the Grenadines. We may have been in the tropics, but you could tell Christmas was just around the corner. There were plenty of tinsel and baubles, and even a few little real fir trees available at vast expense. Not only was I able to get all the fresh produce I wanted, including some local veggies which I was already familiar with from the Grenadines, but I was also able to buy presents for everyone. Christmas was just as it should be – plenty of food and drink, and fun company. The family could not have been more generous with their gifts, and even the kids brought us some lovely and thoughtful presents. If I had to be away from my own family at Christmas, this couldn't have been a better option.

When the family left on 27 December, the boat seemed empty and eerily quiet. That visit was the one and only time we met Claire. I don't think she was that interested in boating. Jules and Claire had recently set up a new hosiery mail order company, and I believe Claire was the main one involved and that obviously took up most of her time. After a mass clean-up below decks, Roy and I turned our heads to making Intrepid even more of a showpiece. Over the next three months, gradually every inch of her beautiful wood shone brightly with several layers of varnish, and the engine room had a thorough clean-up, with Roy spending many hours giving the main engine and generator a complete overhaul in preparation for the big crossing. When a little old local guy asked if we had a job for him, Roy decided to set him to work cleaning all the brass. Wilbur was his name, and every day, five days a week until we left, Wilbur worked from 0800 to 1600 doing nothing but polish brass. He never missed a day, was always prompt and couldn't have been happier, bless him. Just before we left we had Wilbur cover the whole lot with Vaseline to help create a barrier from salt water.

Not long into the New Year, who should we see come staggering into the marina but Laurie Nan, with Captain Kev all dressed up in his whites complete with enough gold braid to think he was an admiral. After our greetings, both Roy and I felt he seemed even more sheepish than the last time we met a few months back in Virginia. We soon found out why once the boat was hauled out. The prop was in a right mess. We never did find out how it happened, but after the prop was replaced with the spare one that all three owners had had the sense to include, they headed back to Florida and the safety of the Intracoastal.

Boots created some amusement for one of our neighbours. He had a habit of checking out any new arrivals, and when this 120-foot powerboat arrived he immediately went up their gangway as soon as it was put out. What he didn't notice was the white poodle sitting at the top, and as soon as the dog spotted Boots, he barked sharply which caused Boots to jump, lose his balance and fall into the water. Like a bat out of hell he immediately sprang back up onto the dock, shaking himself furiously. The crew and I howled with laughter. It really was the funniest thing. A few days later one of the guys came over with another hilarious story about Boots. Quite often he would visit the boat during the evening and be made a big fuss of by the crew. However, the owner's elderly wife did not like cats. Our feline friends seem to sense this, and Boots was no exception. One evening, just as the owner's wife had poured a glass of milk from the fridge, Boots jumped out at her, causing the contents of the glass to be thrown up in the air and then descend straight down all over her head. The crew member who witnessed this had to quickly run forward before his suppressed laughter exploded. The lady was not amused and ordered Boots off the boat, never to return. He, of course, totally ignored this command.

Ideally the best time to do the Atlantic crossing to Europe is around May, before the start of the tropical storms that build up during the summer months. We therefore had plenty of time to prepare, which also enabled us to have plenty of relaxation time socialising with our neighbours. A lovely Canadian family were taking time out living on one of the marina's houseboats. I believe the father had just made a huge profit selling some forestry he owned. There was Mum and Dad, their son and their daughter Paula. We became friends and spent a lot of time together. Although Paula was a year or two younger than me, she was a lot more self-confident and could be quite audacious at times, making me feel somewhat naïve and inadequate. Having a limitless amount of money to spend certainly had a lot to do with it. I remember going to a concert with her to see the pop group Tavares perform. When we got to the venue there was a very long queue. She grabbed my hand and boldly walked right to the front, discreetly handed a bunch of dollars to the doorman that she had at the ready, and we were in. We thoroughly enjoyed the concert and at the end, via one of the venue staff, Paula sent a message to the group inviting them back to the boat for a party. They came, and that was quite a night!

Before Jules left after Christmas, he decided the best way to deal with ship's expenses was to buy some travellers cheques in my name. I can't remember how many dollars' worth he gave me, but I do know it was quite a substantial amount. Paula loved to gamble and enjoyed going in the afternoon when it was quieter and more relaxing. Without too much twisting of arms I found myself joining her on one of these occasions. Roy and I had already been to the casino a few times during the evenings. He would give me $5 to buy five chips whilst he propped up the bar. He reckoned he would have spent that and more on buying me drinks. I occasionally played roulette but, finding that quite boring, most of the time I headed for one of the many blackjack tables. I never came back with any winnings, but playing often kept me amused for a couple of hours or so. Going with Paula was a disaster. I discovered she played a far riskier game than me, often splitting and doubling up. It was exciting to watch, but to my horror I found myself copying her and I soon ran out of chips. I was getting truly hooked and didn't want to stop playing. I started to make use of the traveller's cheques, cashing $50 at a time. Before I realised what I had done, I had spent what was left of them – $300, which, to me, was a lot of money in 1976. Paula didn't seem at all perturbed about it and she had definitely lost a lot more than me. I felt sick and couldn't get out of there quickly enough. I made my excuses to Paula and headed back to the boat. I dreaded telling Roy and, even worse, Jules. He was due to visit us in a few days' time. Roy went very quiet and said it was my problem to sort and certainly for me to tell Jules. I had no savings, and since being with Roy I never really bothered about having money. If I wanted some clothes or something, as long as it was reasonable, Roy would just give me the money. I was mortified by my irresponsible behaviour. As soon as Jules arrived, riddled with guilt and stumbling over the words I told him what I had done. When his face changed expression I thought he was going to explode with anger, but to my surprise and enormous relief he burst out laughing. When I promised I would pay back every cent he brushed it off and said, 'Remind me not to do that again.' I suppose to him $300 was just a drop in the ocean compared to the vast expense of running Intrepid.

Roy had quite a list of spares needed for the boat and came

to the conclusion that it would be a lot cheaper to head over to Fort Lauderdale and collect them making use of both our luggage allowances rather than have them shipped over. It was a lovely, unexpected trip and was further enhanced by flying on a seaplane. Slowly but surely we started to stock the boat up with plenty of spare provisions in preparation for our next long voyage. As we had done on other boats, in the wheelhouse we kept a large, sealed canister full of emergency items with the idea it would be the first thing you would grab should you need to abandon ship and get into the life raft. Not only did it include extra flares but also some fishing tackle, a multipurpose knife set, some light rope, suntan lotion, first aid equipment, sea sickness pills and some glucose sweets. Having recently read 117 Days Adrift, which was about the Baileys and their survival in a dinghy after a whale had sunk their yacht in the Pacific in March 1973, a copy of their book was added to the canister. It is a truly inspirational book on survival. As I was reading their book, I immediately thought about the time on Spirit of Cutty Sark when the whale surfaced right alongside us. I now realised that if it had hit the boat, serious damage would have been done, with a high risk of being holed and possibly sunk.

By the beginning of April we had our crew. There was Grant from Australia, with his local girlfriend Louise, and Gary from New Zealand. They were to come with us as far as Gibraltar. Roy had been keeping a steady eye on the weather patterns in the Atlantic and decided that we could risk leaving a little earlier than planned. So, on 11 April, waving goodbye to all our new-found friends we cast off, our first destination being Bermuda. We soon settled into life at sea and all the crew got on famously. We had a smooth and uneventful passage, arriving on Good Friday to clear customs and immigration in St Georges before moving round to Hamilton. Taking some time out to enjoy Bermuda and, for a change, sorting out just a few maintenance items, we set sail again on 24 April, this time heading for the Azores.

It took twelve days to get there, and along the way we often experienced a large, rolly sea with lots of rain squalls, making it quite uncomfortable on board. To give Boots some relief Gary hung a large basket from one of the beams in the saloon, and that was where Boots spent a lot of his time, gently rocking with the boat motion. The closer we got to the Azores, the more layers of clothes were worn. The temperature was dropping, and we were all having trouble acclimatising to the colder weather. Much to Boots's delight we did manage to catch a few fish, and we were often escorted along the way by a pod of dolphins. We headed for Horta on the island of Faial where we managed to get alongside the main dock, which was perfect as just a few yards down the jetty we were in the small town centre. The Azores are part of Portugal, and I found Horta a fascinating place with so much history from its whaling days. A guy named Anton did scrimshaw using very old whale's teeth. He often sold pieces to Americans but risked about fifty per cent not getting through customs. He carved a picture of Intrepid on one for me, and every time I look at it on my dressing table it brings back such lovely memories of my sailing days. One of the Admiral Cup racing yachts, Noryama, was also tied up along the dock, and we were soon all together, catching up on yachtie news. They too had recently arrived, so we all took the day off to grab some taxis and go sightseeing, taking a picnic with us. It made a nice change to have a few more people to share company with. We visited a place where a volcano erupted in the 1950s, burying a number of villages. It was a vast area of lava rock and it made me shiver at the thought of what lay beneath. America accepted many of the 1,700 people who were displaced.

We were off again on 13 May for our last leg to Europe. We

arrived in the Straits of Gibraltar six days later. As usual, we managed to arrive at our destination in the dark, giving us more of a challenge. This time it was even greater as there were ships going in all directions in this narrow channel. We managed to get through to the duty dockmaster by radio and secured a berth in the destroyer pens in readiness for clearance in the morning. In the middle of breakfast, customs and immigration arrived together and proceeded to clear us into Gibraltar. As soon as they arrived, even though he had not finished his breakfast, Grant disappeared into the forward cabin where he remained until they had left, which I found rather strange. Grant was not one to skip his food and normally was very sociable. It wasn't long before he and Louise shot off, saying they needed to sort out their ongoing travel arrangements. Leaving Gary on board, Roy and I headed off to the post office. Whilst I checked to see if we had any mail, Roy went to telephone Jules to let him know we had arrived safely. I remember sitting on the step outside the post office when I read the sad news contained in a letter from Mum and Dad. They had received a phone call from Mary (Roy's father's partner) who needed our contact details as his father Syd was seriously ill. Assuming we had been contacted, Mum was half expecting to see me as she thought we would be flying straight home after hearing the news, especially so when she then heard he had died. This was obviously news to us. Roy joined me as I was finishing reading the letter, and I handed it over to him. After sitting quietly for a while, he then went off to phone Mary whilst I remained where I was, waiting for him to return. Not being much of a family man, Roy did not see a lot of his father. This was also the case with his son. I was told by his sister on one of our rare visits to the family in Wolverhampton that his mother used to beat him a lot when he was a boy, which I feel sure had a lot to do with it. Apparently Mary had sent a telegram to our address in Nassau which should have arrived a couple of days before we set sail. Sadly, we never received it, but even if we had I am not absolutely sure Roy would have wanted to drop everything and fly home.

After a food shop we returned to the boat, where the three of us had some lunch. A couple of hours later Louise and a very jubilant Grant turned up loaded with parcels. There was a portable DC TV for Roy and a battery-run turntable for me. Wow, that was a surprise. He said it was a big thank you, and before we knew it their bags were packed and they were shaking our hands saying goodbye, leaving us quite overwhelmed with the generosity of the gifts and surprised at the suddenness of their departure. It wasn't until some years later that the penny dropped for me. Just before leaving Nassau, two gentlemen came to speak to Grant. Standing on the dock wearing black suits, they stood out like sore thumbs. When I questioned who they were, Grant said they were something to do with one of Louise's clients. And his being so evasive when the custom and immigration officers were clearing us into Gibraltar made me realise that Grant was probably up to something. It wouldn't have been drugs as, with Algiers close by, it would have been like taking coal to Newcastle. Was it money laundering? Paradise Island was well known as a mafia base, and they had their quick getaway boat moored close by us. Buying those gifts was definitely a bit over the top. A touch of guilt, perhaps? Another thought also struck me: was that telegram deliberately held back to avoid any delay in leaving, or am I being too cynical? We shall never know for sure.

Within the destroyer pens there were a lot of visiting yachts, and it wasn't long before Boots got into trouble again. As Roy and I, along with some newly made friends, were enjoying evening drinks on the aft deck, two guys came along with an Alsatian dog on a lead. 'Excuse me,' they said, 'would you mind keeping your cat away from our dog?' We all burst into laughter, but they assured us that they were very serious. Apparently, the dog was completely intimidated by Boots's stalking. Brave, but what a naughty puss he was becoming! There was also another mishap with my leg whilst in Gibraltar. On my way back to the boat on one of the bikes, with a full gas bottle on the front and clean laundry tied to the rear, my wooden foot suddenly slipped off the pedal and I only just managed to stop before falling off. I discovered the foot had once again gone all floppy. I had to pedal like mad with the good foot whilst keeping the other foot slightly up in the air. When Roy took it apart this time it was the actual rocker movement that had rusted apart. He decided to make use of his naval background and went off to the dockyard to see what could be done. In an economy drive, the navy had disposed of having a permanent maintenance crew on every ship, and instead a team would travel around to each dock when one of the vessels had a reasonable list of defects. Good news – the boys were in town. In no time at all they managed to copy the broken one but using stainless steel instead of ordinary steel. From then onwards I made sure that ankle joint was used on all my replacement legs until that system became obsolete.

Yet again we were featured in the local newspaper – the Gibraltar Chronicle – which meant we received plenty of curious visitors. That boat was even better than having a new baby for making friends quickly, and as Roy and I both loved meeting new people, we were always very welcoming. Intrepid quickly became the hub of life in the destroyer pens. A week later Gary finally left to return to New Zealand to complete his degree course. He was such a great guy: always polite, never lost his temper and quietly got on with his duties on board – an excellent crew member. We had about a week of pottering on the boat along with lots of socialising before Jules arrived with a new girlfriend in tow. Julia was her name, and I have to say I am not sure Jules deserved her – she was such a lovely, gentle lady. Jules was in an excellent mood. An associate of his was convinced that Intrepid would not make it across the pond; so much so that he made a bet – which of course he lost. It must have been substantial as Jules decided to spend the winnings on hiring a Spanish finca (farmhouse) up in the hills above Estepona, just along the coast from Gibraltar, for us all to have four days of relaxation. He had even hired a local chef to look after the four of us. Life was getting better every day!

So, on 10 June we said goodbye to Gib and motored around the corner to the marina at Puerto Banús, where we secured the boat and grabbed a taxi to our holiday home for the next four days. I found it so very relaxing being up in the hills, enjoying the magnificent views, and eating and drinking far too much. It was so peaceful and I loved hearing the chirping of birds instead of the squawking of seagulls. On the second day, in a somewhat inebriated state, we all decided we just had to go to a bullfight. None of us had experienced this Spanish tradition, and in high spirits we set off the following day to one being held in Algeciras. We fully embraced the festival atmosphere when we arrived, but once the picadors on the horses started to use their lances on the bull, all four of us became quieter and quieter, and by the time the matadors were strutting around the ring we had had enough and headed back to the hire car. It wasn't until we were about halfway back to the finca that we were able to talk about it. We all felt quite sickened at the cruelty of it, and agreed that no way could it be described as a sport. I suppose it is a bit like our own tradition of fox hunting. Over time these types of so-called sport will become unacceptable.

Ibiza was our next destination and we arrived on 17 June. As there was no room for us at the marina, we anchored in the outer harbour and used our dory to get ashore via the inner harbour which was incredibly polluted. Every time I went ashore there, I used to take a deep breath and hold it for as long as possible whilst quickly tying up the boat and jumping ashore. It was such a disgusting smell, most of which I am sure came from raw sewage. Having said that, once ashore, Ibiza was an exciting and vibrant place to be. There was nothing better than sitting in one of the open-air restaurants in the centre, having a coffee whilst watching the young elite of Europe showing off. It was in the days of espadrilles with shirts over bikinis, tied with belts, and flimsy, colourful wrap-around dresses which both Julia and I bought with very little delay. Jules fell in love with the place; so much so that apart from one or two trips to the other Balearic Islands, Ibiza was our base until it was time for Jules and Julia to return to the States. He even employed a young Spanish chef and his English girlfriend to work on the boat so that he and Julia could enjoy more of our company. How about that! By the time they left it was too late in the season to carry on to the Greek Islands. Ah well, another time perhaps. Once Roy and I were back on our own, we spent a lot of our time anchored off the smaller island of Formentera where we enjoyed swimming in the beautifully clear bay. We shared the bay with two other yachts. One was German and the other was Spanish, and I believe there was a royal prince on board although this was never confirmed. We often shared company in the evening, taking turns to supply supper. We were now treading water, so to speak, until the end of the summer when it would be time to head back the way we came.

CHAPTER 17 – HOMEWARD BOUND

Whilst Jules was with us Roy showed him how bad the electrics were. The Chinese wiring used when it was built in 1969 was of very poor quality and was forever breaking, causing all sorts of problems. It was therefore agreed that we would take the boat to Cowes on the Isle of Wight, to the same boatyard we were in with Atlast, for a major electrical refit before returning to the States. This was fantastic news as it meant not only would we be able to catch up with all our UK mates, but also I would get to spend some time with my family whilst we waited for the right weather conditions for yet another Atlantic crossing. We left for a return visit to Gibraltar on 27 August, arriving back in the destroyer pens four days later. After restocking the boat and catching up with some of our new-found Gibraltarian friends, which included a few visits to our favourite little restaurant, Jim's Den, we set sail for dear ol' England on 8 September with two additional crew members – two young guys, Dave and Pete, who were looking for a working passage back to England. Once again we chose well as they proved to be excellent crew.

It took longer than expected to reach Cowes as we had a few delays en route. It was a wet, cold and rolly trip for most of the way, so we spent a night in Bayonne and another in Coruna along the Spanish Atlantic coast before crossing the Bay of

Biscay. Once in the English Channel we headed to Alderney, where we spent two days as a special request from me. It was once again my birthday, and I wanted to celebrate it with some French food ashore. When we reached the Needles Channel, Roy alerted the port authorities that we required clearance and that we had a cat on board. We were immediately refused entry to Cowes and had to go to a designated buoy in Southampton Water, where we awaited a visit from a Port Health Official. Dearie me, what a fuss was made over poor old Boots. We knew he would need to go into quarantine, but had no idea what a performance and expense it would end up being. In order to allow Boots to be transported to a cattery on the mainland we needed a special licence that could only be obtained from London, which we had to have couriered down to avoid any further delay. I was so sad as I said goodbye to Boots, and his protest meowing was heart-wrenching. We would be parted for roughly two months. We arrived at the boatyard in Cowes late the following day, and I immediately phoned Mum and Dad to let them know I was back in England. I couldn't wait to see them so I shot home a couple of days later, leaving Roy to organise the work that needed to be done on the boat. I spent a glorious, luxurious week wallowing in Mum's fussing and excellent cooking. What bliss! It doesn't matter how old you are – for me, anyway – it's lovely being treated like a little girl again, but there is a limit. At the age of twenty-eight, being reminded to take a coat when going out became rather tiresome. All said and done, I loved them to bits and have always felt extremely fortunate that I was bought up in such a loving, close family.

The electrical refit was progressing well, and although we had left Jules a few messages giving updates, we had not heard back from him. Knowing how much he loved England we were expecting him to descend upon us at any time. Towards the end of October we received a message from our old friend Frank

Atlas in Fort Lauderdale, asking us to call him back. As we guessed that Frank was trying to reach us about a job he had for us, his news was even more of a shock. Jules had sold the boat, and the new owner was a guy called Jack Roberts who would be in touch with us shortly. We were so surprised and certainly didn't see this coming. Jules never so much as hinted he was thinking of selling Intrepid when we were together in the Balearics. Maybe he had already put Intrepid on the market by then, hence the reason why he was insistent we spent so much time together rather than working on the boat. We had so many unanswered questions, none of which Frank was able to shed any light on. Was the running of the boat getting too expensive, or was he under pressure from Claire to sell? Perhaps she got wind of Julia, and Jules wanted to save the marriage. We will never know the reason why he sold. And that was it; we never saw or spoke to Jules again. A few years ago, I idly googled Jules's name and couldn't believe what I found out from more than one news report. It was such sad reading. In 1980 Claire and Jules broke up their twenty-five-year marriage with Claire getting a $1.8 million settlement from the hosiery business. The split was not altogether a surprise to me, but I was certainly impressed with how fast the business had taken off. What was really sad was that just three years later, at the age of only fifty-six, Jules died of heart disease, leaving his whole estate to his young adopted son, twenty-two-year old Bryan, including ninety-seven per cent of the hosiery business which was generating $100 million sales on an annual basis. Even sadder, seven years later Bryan died from a bee sting. He had only been married for a few months, and having no children created a two-year legal battle over the estate between Claire, the new wife and his other adopted son Jeff. In one of the reports I read it said that Jules came from a poor immigrant family, so he somehow managed to make quite a lot of money before starting the hosiery business, and it had to have been quite substantial in order to buy Intrepid and afford the cost of running her, including paying our wages. I do recollect that Jules once muttered something about being involved with the garbage business in Philadelphia, which begs the question: was he really teasing about the gunrunning to Cuba?

Sure enough, Jack contacted us the following day and said he would be over to see us in three days' time. Both Roy and I felt a little anxious and hoped we would get on all right. We also had no idea what his intentions were regarding the boat. Was he expecting us to bring Intrepid back to the States, and if so, would it be just a delivery and would we be looking for another job because he already had his own crew? There was also the question of Boots. We need not have worried. Jack was a smallish guy with a full beard and, coming from Atlanta, Georgia, spoke with a southern drawl. He came in tow with a much younger girl called Steph. I say girl, because whilst Jack was well into his forties, I reckon Steph was around twenty. They were both a little dumpy and very chirpy. Almost the first words we heard from Steph were: 'Jack, eat shit!' Not very pleasant, but that was Americans for you, and as it was her favourite expression, we soon got used to hearing it. The good news was that Jack had no intention of letting us go, and he wanted the boat brought back to the States. And what really put a smile on my face was that he had no problem with Boots. Phew! So, as far as we were concerned, nothing had really changed, and Jack seemed to be an okay guy to work for and appeared to be financially sound.

Work on Intrepid was finally completed at the beginning of December, which was excellent timing weather-wise for the crossing. On one of our visits home we met up with Michael White in our local pub, the Black Bull. He was the one who came with us on the catamaran delivery to California, and through him we met Michael Bunting, known as Bunny. By the end of the evening we had persuaded him to join us. That made two extra crew as we had already agreed to include a friend of ours, Olivia. She had recently gone through a divorce, resulting in her ex-husband having custody of their two little girls, and needed to have some time out doing something different. The crossing sure ticked the box for her. It was also good news for me to have another girl on board, especially as she was very happy to do most of the cooking. This would then free me up to do more navigating under Roy's guidance, which I was really keen to do. And finally, two guys – Andy and Paul from Tasmania, Australia – joined us, making a total of six, which was ideal. With two sharing a night watch, the rest of the crew would get to sleep for four hours at a time – such luxury.

When it came time to leave on 11 December, Roy requested if Boots could be transported to the island to avoid us having to go across to the mainland which would result in us missing the tide. We finally got the message that the owner of the cattery was allowed to bring him across on the ferry, provided he was in a secure cage and escorted by a policeman, and then met on arrival by another policeman who would then escort said lady and cat to the boat, where customs and immigration officers would be waiting. Boots would then be put in a place that required two doors to be opened with a sign on each saying 'cat in quarantine'. Once this had all happened, the two officers then sat down with relief in the saloon to complete all the paperwork. When they produced the thick file for Intrepid they explained that if ever a complicated clearance case was required for training purposes, our boat would be the one to use. Apparently, the decision on how Boots was to be moved had escalated up the line until it hit the home secretary's desk. How ridiculous! Added to that, the boat was registered in Panama, we carried excess booze which had to be bonded, the crew were foreign, and we had claimed zero-rated VAT for the work that had been done.

When the officers left, one of them spotted a cat at the end of the pontoon.

'Isn't that your cat?' he said.

Quick as a flash, Andy said, 'Ah, no mate. That one has got quite different markings.' With a shrug they left. Phew! It was of course Boots. He had climbed out of the open porthole and managed to clamber over the boat onto the dock. When I grabbed him he wouldn't stop licking my face and making little mewing noises telling me how happy he was to be back. We really missed each other, and it was so good to have our final crew member back on board.

At 1300 we slipped our lines, waving to everyone who had come to say goodbye. Quite a few of Olivia's family, including her two little girls, had also come along to see her off. It made me think about my own mum and dad. They had never come to see me off or even asked whether they could. When I think of Mum and Dad whilst away, I see them comfortably at home and not standing on a dock waving goodbye. I am not superstitious, but as this had never happened, I would not want this to change. Each time I did a crossing, the more anxious I became, especially during the preparation time and for at least the first couple of days at sea. I would mentally go through the lists trying to think of anything vital I had forgotten, but thankfully this never happened. By the third day I would become a lot more settled and begin to relax into life at sea and all that it threw at us.

Oh yes, back to Boots. Once in the English Channel, Roy decided to check the radar was working properly. Unbeknownst to us Boots was sitting on top of the scanner. As soon as it started to spin, it shot him off into the sea. Thank God Mike saw him go. I shouted to him not to take his eyes off him whilst we quickly turned the boat around, and was able to scoop him up with the fish net. That was the closest we came to losing him. If the channel had been any rougher, we would never have found him.

As soon as we got going, Andy became seriously seasick. He stayed below, hanging onto the foremast, which was not good news. I was getting really worried as he couldn't keep anything down and was even bringing up the water I managed to get him to drink. On the third day, in desperation I made an egg and milk drink, gave him Valium to calm him down and managed to get him up on the aft deck in the fresh air. It took another couple of days before he started to properly improve, which was a great relief to us all. By then Roy and I had decided that Andy would have to leave us at our next port of call. We just couldn't take the risk of him being so seasick all the way across the Atlantic. On 20 December we arrived in Funchal in Madeira for a very quick stop so that I could pick up a turkey at the English supermarket. I wasn't sure I would be able to get one once we arrived at Tenerife, where we intended to spend Christmas and sit it out until the trade winds kicked in. Mission accomplished, we left beautiful Madeira the following day, arriving in Tenerife via an overnight stop in Las Palmas on 23 December. By then Andy was greatly improved, and against our better judgement he persuaded us not to let him go. As it turned out, from then onwards Andy was a fantastic crew member and was never sick again.

With Olivia's help we did ourselves proud in producing a great Christmas spread. I had already done a Christmas cake and pud, and thanks to the amazing Spanish market there was plenty of fresh produce. Drinks started early on Christmas Day, and in a very joyous mood Roy and Mike went off in the dory to invite all visiting yachts for a party on Intrepid later on. Both Olivia and I were not too happy about this, so we took ourselves off after our scrumptious turkey lunch to spend some quieter time and have a swim with a family we had met who were renting a villa. When we arrived back in the early evening the party was in full swing, but there was no sign of Roy. I discovered him fast asleep in the cabin. By about midnight I had had enough and decided everyone should go home, which was quite a challenge as by then many were drunk. At least two guys fell in trying to get into their dinghies, and one German guy donated all his CDs to the depths of the harbour, which was a great pity. The boat was in such a mess. Someone had lit candles and stuck them on the varnished services on the aft deck, leaving a few burns and plenty of wax to scrape away. I was furious. How could someone do that? The following day Olivia and I left the cleaning up to the guys whilst we went off to calm down and relax ashore. Everything was shipshape upon our return; we received plenty of apologies, and they even cooked supper for us.

As we would be motoring a lot more than the rest of the yachts, we were the first to leave on 10 January 1977, with the hope we would soon run into the trade winds. We departed to a very loud fanfare of hooters from all the other boats. Next stop Barbados. It wasn't long before Andy caught a small fish for Boots and immediately became his best friend. Five days later as the wind veered round, we decided to heave-to rather than sail miles off course. That night we rolled around whilst thunder and lightning passed over us. It took a couple more days before the trades settled down enough for us to make good progress. Ten days later, Boots got his first flying fish. Early that morning on his way back from his litter box, which was housed in a little shelter on the foredeck, he spotted it. According to Roy, he came rushing into the wheelhouse with it in his mouth, dropped it on the floor, loudly meowed and did a very happy leap in the air. As we'd discovered previously, when flying fish are disturbed they would leap up and then hit one of the sails, ending up stunned on deck. This mostly happened at night. From then onwards Boots would regularly patrol the decks a number of times, day and night. We hardly had to supplement his fish diet.

Nineteen days after leaving Tenerife, on 6 February 1977 we arrived in Barbados, once again bang on target with the navigation. Well done, Roy. I also did quite a lot of noon sights using the old plastic sextant whilst Roy used his smart brass one. I was really chuffed to find that most times my position was pretty close to his. I just love playing with figures and looked forward to doing this exercise most days. To produce a noon sight you do of course need to see the sun, which wasn't always possible. It was therefore very important that all crew logged the speed and compass direction on an hourly basis. We didn't stay for long, and left Barbados on 5 February for beautiful Bequia. I just couldn't wait to return. The closer we got, the more excited I became. It really was, and still is, my absolute favourite Caribbean island. On the spur of the moment Roy decided to stop overnight at Mustique beforehand. It was Andy's birthday, and everyone was wanting to see what was becoming quite a celebrity island. For me, it was very strange returning to the scene of my accident. I was full of mixed feelings but surprisingly found they were not so sad. I never really suffered from huge regrets and questions of 'if only' regarding my accident. It happened, that was that, and I just got on with my life, making the most of it. I was more curious to see how much more of the island had been developed over the past six years. It was all beginning to look very impressive, and Basil's Bar was up and running by then. The wreck of the SS Antilles was now very rusty, lying there in two parts. It brought back memories of that poor distressed captain sitting on the deck of Cutty Sark, repeatedly saying in his heavy French accent that the rock was not charted. I wonder if that was the end of his career.

The following morning we motored over to Bequia, anchoring for lunch in Friendship Bay before going round to Port Elizabeth. As we entered the bay, I caught my breath. I had forgotten how truly beautiful it was; so much so, I had tears in my eyes and just stood there, taking it all in. The sparkling blue of the bay, the bleached white sand of Princess Margaret beach and the palm tree-lined coastline. As we motored further into the bay, I could see the colourful bougainvillea around the Frangipani Hotel and the brightly painted little wooden buildings lining the main street. And as I breathed in deeply, I caught that magical and unique, indescribable scent of fragrant flowers mixed with a hint of coconuts, bananas and fish, with the smell of the lush, tropical greenery that lay just a little further inland. As soon as we dropped anchor, I dived into the deliciously warm, clear water and just floated. I was in seventh heaven in a place that will always have a little of my heart. Arrangements were soon made for Olivia and Mike's return to the UK, and for Andy and Paul to head back to Australia. We left for St Vincent five days later, where we had a great reunion with all our Vincentian friends, revisiting the Cobblestone Inn in town and enjoying our rum drinks at the Mariners Inn; but it was also time to say goodbye to our brilliant crew. When I gave Olivia a hug little did I know that two years later she would be one of the nineteen people who lost their lives in the disastrous Fastnet Race back in England, along with her boyfriend, John, who was also a friend of ours.

As soon as we arrived in Bequia, Roy contacted the owner, Jack, and it was arranged that he and his family would join the boat in St Lucia on 6 March for a sailing trip to Antigua. So we decided to take a few well-earned days off first, revisiting some of our other favourite Grenadine islands. First stop was Tobago

Cays where we enjoyed some wonderful snorkelling. I never stopped marvelling at the mass of colour that opens up once that mask goes on and you look below the surface. For a long period of time I just floated around, completely lost in watching hundreds of brightly coloured tropical fish flitting in and out of the stunning coral reef habitat that surrounds this group of little islands. The following day we motored over to Palm Island. Most of the building work had been completed, and now that all the colourful planting had matured, the island was looking absolutely stunning. It was obvious that the Caldwells had not been idle over the past few years, and it was lovely catching up with them even though John became very agitated on seeing Boots with us. He was so very protective of the local wildlife, particularly the birds and the turtles. We only stayed for lunch before going across to Union Island for the evening, where anchoring was a lot safer. Next stop was Petit St Vincent to catch up with Hayes. As soon as any of the staff recognised us, they shouted 'Cutty Sark'. They still remembered us winning the Bequia–St Vincent races seven years previously. The bartender, Goatie, said that he loved seeing Spirit of Cutty Sark anchored off the island as it was his favourite yacht. He has now retired, and you will find the beach bar has been named after him.

Once back in Bequia, Roy and I tackled the inevitable long list of things to do before setting off to St Lucia, the next island north of St Vincent. Before picking the family up in Castries, we spent the night in Marigot Bay on the western end of St Lucia. It is one of only a few hurricane holes where yachts run to for safety when the wind gets up. It is said that the whole British fleet hid from the French there back in the 1700s, disguising the tops of their masts with palm fronds. That night, safely tucked up in bed, Roy and I were awoken by some very loud squawking. We rushed up on deck and were met by the sight of Boots frantically hanging onto the tail end of a pelican, looking like he was about to take off into the air with the enormous bird. I shouted at him to let go. He was so startled that for once he did as he was told. That cat was something else!

We had a really fun time with Jack and his three boys – Jack Jnr, John and George. Once again we had teenagers on board, and we loved their energy and enthusiasm. As we gradually got to know Jack, we found him great company, and it was obvious he was thoroughly enjoying his new acquisition. En route to Antigua we stopped at Pigeon Island, and then continued on to Martinique and its amazing French market. We cruised our way up through Dominica and Guadeloupe, and finally arrived in Antigua on 20 March. Thanks to Jack's generosity we sampled some excellent Caribbean food along the way. Fried plantain with fresh fish is hard to beat. I absolutely love trying out local food, and picked up some great ideas on what to do with some of the strange-looking vegetables I had seen in the markets but had yet to try. Before departing we received our sailing orders from Jack. We were to bring the boat up to New England for the summer when the boys would join us for part of their school holidays, along with himself for some of the time. Once again, there were big grins all round.

Chapter 18 – End of an Era

We arrived in Antigua shortly before the annual race week. What excellent timing. This was originally started in 1968 by a few charter yachts of various sizes. The idea was for everyone to let their hair down and have some fun at the end of the season. Over the years it has become more and more serious, with yachts now travelling some distance to compete. You will not see water-bomb fights or a greased-up piglet running around on one of the decks as a deterrent to winning one of the races these days. Nelson's Dockyard in English Harbour was for many years the place you headed for to have any serious work done on your boat, especially at the end of the season before either going north to the States or over to Europe for the summer. It included an essential slipway. Nicholson's boatyard, headed by Commander Nicholson, had been established there since the 1950s. The dock was always a hive of activity with plenty of work in progress going on. Many of the charter boats based there rented one of the old officers' quarters for storage. They were built in the 1700s during Nelson's time. Jack didn't need persuading to spend money on Intrepid to keep her in tip-top condition, so there was quite a list for the boatyard to tackle. We had all the interior carved wood revarnished, and after two Atlantic crossings, all of Wilbur's hard work of polishing the brass on deck needed redoing, along with the varnishing all of the exterior teak wood. We also made good use of the slipway by having the hull antifouled. Once the work was complete we moved Intrepid across the bay to the marina, just in time before race week started. Let the fun begin! Whilst socialising in the Admirals Inn, Roy got talking to the Bermudan race team, and with some persuasion he agreed to be their sailing master. They had never won a medal, but they reckoned with Roy's guidance they stood a good chance.

As for me, I had the surprise of my life. Friends Ken and Fran Mackenzie owned the magnificent 72 ft ketch Ticonderoga, affectionally known as Big Ti. She was built in 1936 and was a world-renowned racer when in her prime. It had become a tradition that for the final race to Guadeloupe, Ken had an all-girl crew. He asked me to helm. 'Me?' I squeaked. He assured me that he would be right behind me sitting on the aft rail, telling me what to do. In trepidation I agreed, and had a sleepless night thinking about what I had let myself in for. The start of that race I shall never forget, and it remains one of my most memorable moments of sailing. With the usual brisk trade winds blowing, there were yachts jostling for position in all directions, with dramatic tacking and jibing and shouting going on. Knowing every inch of the boat, Fran was in charge of the deck, and as promised, Ken sat right behind me on the aft rail. Up till then I hadn't even been behind Big Ti's wheel, yet alone race her. I had no idea how she would respond to my steering. My heart was in my mouth as I concentrated hard on doing exactly what Ken bellowed at me to do. We tacked and jibed like the rest of the fleet, and as the gun went off, with Ken's amazing expertise we were first over the line and away, with the sails beautifully trimmed. How those girls managed the frantic deck work was unbelievable. It was true 'girl power' and of course we won the race. As for Roy, for the first time ever the Bermudan team achieved a bronze medal. Roy was their hero.

That year – 1977 – Nelson's Dockyard was to be closed down as a boatyard and reopened as a museum. So, after race week everything had to be cleared out of the officers' quarters in readiness for the Antiguan government to commence the restoration work. It was the end of an era for one of the grotty yachties' favourite gathering places. The occasion was marked in the only way that it could have been – a party to end all parties; and boy, it was just that. There was a body-painting theme of food, and clothing had to be minimal. I went as rhubarb and custard but cannot think what the hell Roy went as. He had splodges of paint all over him. The rum flowed and there were lots of non-stop music jam sessions. It lasted for three days! On the last day, a group including Roy decided to escort one of the girls to the airport. All they did was don a layer of clothing over all the paint. Those at the airport must have been quite disturbed at seeing a scruffy rabble of somewhat drunken people making so much noise in saying goodbye to one of their passengers.

During the party, at one stage I desperately wanted some sleep and decided to go back to the boat for a few hours. In my very drunken state I climbed down into our dory, but I couldn't start the electric outboard motor. So I decided to do it manually. This was never easy for me, and in order to gain enough purchase I had to put my good foot on the side of the dory transom before pulling the cord. The good news was that I succeeded in starting the engine, but in the process I lost balance when letting go of the cord and shot straight over the outboard into the water. Luckily it was just water I hit. Surfacing, I managed to find my leg, which had come off, throw it into the dory and somehow clamber back into the boat. Motoring across the pitch-black bay without any mishap had to have been pure luck as there were lots of floating buoys, not to mention the many yachts at anchor. The next morning I found myself in my bed with a very soggy leg by my side. I had lost the stump sock when I fell in, so I must have managed to climb onto Intrepid one-legged while carrying my artificial one. Thank goodness I still had the stainless steel ankle joint, which had been transferred to my new leg which had been made before leaving England. As the stump alters shape over the years, replacement legs are regularly needed. Just a slight change can cause chafing, and in no time at all you become immobilised and truly qualify as a disabled person.

On 2 June we said goodbye to Antigua and headed for Bermuda. We had three additional crew members – Richard, Lisa and Jennie, who were all friends. They came from Vermont and were hoping for a sailing trip back. It was an uneventful six-day journey except that the day before arrival the heat exchanger on the main engine broke. We managed to limp our way into St Georges where we were cleared before moving round to Hamilton. I was hoping we would be able to spend a little time on the island as I really loved Bermuda, and was therefore disappointed when Roy said we could only stay for one night as we needed to press on. Thanks to having to wait for a replacement heat exchanger to come from the States we ended up being there for thirteen days. Tee hee, I was one happy girl. Due to being a small but busy island you were only allowed one car per family. It was therefore the norm for the wife to have the car whilst her husband used a moped. I found it highly amusing to sit on deck watching Hamilton's rush hour – lots of mopeds driven by city gentlemen in their jackets and smart Bermudan shorts, hanging onto their briefcases. Some even wore bowler hats.

Once the Bermudan race team heard we were in town they treated us like royalty. They were all influential guys so we ended up attending many cocktail parties. It was rather like stepping back a couple of decades. There, casual meant a cravat and jacket rather than a suit. Once again Roy and I found ourselves somewhat underdressed, but it was all great fun and we were truly spoilt by their hospitality. We spent a memorable day at the house of one of the racing guys who was Portuguese and had made a small fortune building swimming pools in Bermuda. We dived for calico clams in a bay close by, and once they'd been dumped in ice water to clear them of sand they were popped onto a barbecue. I had never tasted anything so exquisite, especially when dipped in melted garlic butter. To this day I can still remember that delicious taste. On leaving, the guy gave us a huge jar of traditional Bermudan pickled onions, for which they are famous. I believe he called them 'argus apples'. They certainly lived up to their reputation, and we enjoyed them for months afterwards.

The next stop was Newport, Rhode Island, which took five days. The day before we entered American waters Roy gave the order for the crew to dispose of any joints they had left. The crew were okay, I suppose, but I was not happy that they smoked pot. Although I had also smoked on occasions, I was not really that fussed and much preferred alcohol for getting high, and certainly not at sea. Drugs were never my scene. There was a ceremonious dumping at sea. Just before entering port I did my usual thing of tidying up the boat. On going into the forward cabin to collect any rubbish, I found one of the girls stitching some pot into one of her tampons. I was so mad I turned back and told Roy to sort her out. If customs had found any drugs on board, Roy's career as a skipper would have been at serious risk. Richard was a good guy, but I have to say I was not too impressed with the girls and was quite relieved to wave them goodbye soon after arrival at Newport.

After a week spent enjoying this lovely town once again, we headed off to Egertown in Martha's Vineyard where we were to be based for the rest of the summer, arriving on 8 July in good time before Jack and the boys were due to join us. What a beautiful town. It was full of lovely old colonial wooden buildings, and everywhere was immaculate. It is well known for being the place that many of the elite go for their summer holidays and therefore an expensive place to be. It also gained notoriety over the Ted Kennedy incident when he drove his car off the Chappaquiddick Bridge, causing his lady passenger to drown. Roy and I just had to walk over that bridge, and Boots came too.

Just before the family descended upon us, we had a delivery of two brand new laser dinghies. Jack had asked if Roy would teach the boys to dinghy sail, and these were the boats Roy recommended. It was certainly a fun summer with the boys on board, along with Jack and Steph joining us for long weekends. The laser dinghies were well and truly used, and by the end of the summer all three boys were competent sailors. Roy and I also used them a lot and entered a few local races. He did us proud by winning most of the time, and by literally following him, I managed a second and third place. At the end of the summer both lasers were given to us as a thank you for looking after the kids so well. How generous was that!

Jack loved to cook, and when he discovered I had a set of illustrated international cookbooks along with my treasured copy of Larousse Gastronomique, he zoomed in on the classic French recipes. We ended up spending many happy hours putting together some rather complex dishes which took ages to prepare and by contrast were devoured in no time at all. Saddle of Veal Orloff complete with all the trimmings was a particularly spectacular effort. No expense was spared. If a dish required a few slithers of truffle, then a jar of them would be bought at vast expense. In one of our favourite restaurants, at an allotted time the waiters and waitresses would stop serving and put on a small musical show. It was really impressive and we loved the songs, which we had not heard before. It was some time later that we realised the music came from the movie Grease. I have no idea if they were part of the cast, or perhaps understudies or extras, but they knew the moves and sang the songs well. We were sad once the boys left to return home. Jack and Steph then came for the weekend, but, without warning us, Jack dumped Steph. The first we knew about it was when we heard Steph howling as Jack took off, leaving us to deal with a very emotional young lady displaying the Italian part of her heritage. Several hours passed before she managed to calm down. I was so disappointed at the way Jack chose to do it and felt very sorry for Steph, who was obviously devastated at losing him.

Now summer was drawing to an end, it was time to turn south, and once again we were heading back to Fort Lauderdale. Before leaving New England, Roy and I sailed over to Nantucket. We were both fascinated with the whaling history, especially knowing how it was done back in Bequia, and spent long periods of time in the museums. The marina in Nantucket was huge, so there was no problem finding space for Intrepid. It was there that we bumped into an old friend of ours, Hans Hoffman, who skippered Fandango. Hans was born in East Berlin and, as a young man, managed to escape into the West. The last time we saw him was in Antigua at the party. That evening Boots didn't return home, which was a first. We were supposed to leave the following day but delayed going for a further two days. Even after searching around the marina and asking every single person we saw, there was still no sign of Boots. By then I was getting seriously upset and concerned. We decided that Roy would continue onto Newport, and as Hans was also heading in the same direction two days later, I would stay on Fandango so that I could do a thorough search of the whole area and get some posters printed and displayed with the hope of finding him. That evening the three of us went ashore for supper, and on our way back to the marina I was bemoaning the loss of Boots. 'Boots, Boots, where are you?' I called out. All of a sudden there was a meow, and out he popped from behind some bushes. What luck! I was overjoyed at finding him, and judging by the amount of licking from Boots, he was also relieved at finding me. He had a habit of trying to follow us, so we would often put him down below to give us time to shoot off before he managed to return to the dock. I reckon he tried to follow us and, due to the size of the marina, lost his bearings when trying to return to the boat.

We arrived back in Newport on 26 August, and as it turned out, we were there for just under a month as Jack wanted to spend some time with us there. Once again we hit the local news. This time it was for being the flagship for the Mount Gay Rum Trophy race which was then, I believe, specifically for wooden boats over 50 ft. We even had a miniature brass cannon as the starting gun, which sounded impressively loud when Roy fired it off. The deck was swarming with lots of jacketed gentlemen with clipboards, and I played hostess with trays of drinks and snacks. All rather amusing. We were moored not far from Enterprise, one of the contenders for the America's Cup race which was happening whilst we were there. We met up socially with a lot of teams including the notorious Ted Turner. Skippering Courageous, he knocked out all the other defenders including Enterprise, and beat the winning challenger Australia to win the cup. As you can imagine, Newport was bursting at the seams with the sailing fraternity and onlookers watching this incredible contest unfold. What good timing for us to be there at such an exciting time. We were also able to catch up with Ken and Fran, who at that time lived in Newport. Fran was heavily pregnant with her first child and I was invited to her baby shower, an event that was new to me. Not really having a clue what to buy for the baby-to-be, I went into a pharmacy, picked up a nappy bin and went around the shelves, filling it up with all sorts of baby paraphernalia and popping a small teddy bear on the top. Fran was well impressed with my knowledge – ha ha!

Once again I was able to celebrate my birthday in Newport before we carried on south on 24 September. Almost repeating our previous trip, which included enjoying the sights of New York, we stopped in Philadelphia on the evening of 30 September with the hope of catching up with Jules. Unfortunately, he must have been out of town as we couldn't reach him, even though we hung around for a few days. We were on a dock close to the tugboats and were glad that we had Boots. We found the remains of at least three rats on the deck. Boots had eaten their bodies but left their heads and their furry balls. Ugh! It was time for deworming. As they were very curious, Roy showed the Polish tug drivers around the boat, and in return they invited us to join them for supper. They had obviously made an effort to clean up the inside of the tug and even managed to find a tablecloth. It was a great evening, and we came away full of delicious Polish sausage and some rather sweet liquor that turned out to have quite a kick.

When we arrived in Annapolis in the second week of October, I had decided that I needed a break on my own. For some time I had been getting restless and starting to question what I wanted in life. I was now twenty-nine, and looking back, I believe I was getting broody. I knew that as far as Roy was concerned, no way did he want to start a new family, and to be quite honest, I don't think I wanted that with Roy and the style of living we had either. But what did I want? I decided to spend some time on my own to think things through. I hired a car and drove off to visit various people I knew who didn't live too far away. This included spending some time with Jack in Atlanta. By then we were quite comfortable with each other and able to have a heart-to-heart conversation, which helped. I also spent time with Ken and Fran back in Newport. By then Fran had had the baby – a little girl they named Margaret. I then drove up into the hills of Vermont where our ex-crew member Richard lived. Being autumn, the scenery was breathtaking. I had never seen so many shades of brown, red and gold in so many magnificent trees. There was a constant fluttering of leaves dropping to the ground, covering the surface with this beautiful array of colours. It was so magical.

Staying with Richard was a real insight for me to see how a different group of people lived. He owned a large, rambling house that he shared with six or seven others who were a little younger and waiting for the ski season to kick in. In the meantime they were all on social security and spent their money on drugs. I just couldn't understand why Richard put up with them. They even stole two rings of mine. They were only costume jewellery but they had sentimental value. One was made of abalone shell and was given to me by Lavinia after my accident. That one did eventually get returned after Richard intervened. I have to say though, once they realised I wasn't into drugs I was never under pressure to take any. I felt like a fly on the wall observing their day-to-day way of life. For breakfast it was pot, and as the day progressed, stronger drugs were taken. By the evening, apart from Richard they were completely stoned. What a mess. What a life to live. He wanted me to stay a little longer, but after a few days I was more than ready to move on.

Two weeks later I was back on the boat and had made my decision. Once we got to Fort Lauderdale, I was going to leave Roy and return home to England. This may sound crazy to many, but I wanted a normal life, a nine-to-five job and a mortgage. I wanted stability and – a bit silly, I know – a dressing table that I could put things on knowing they would stay put. I needed to prove that I could survive on my own, and hopefully, eventually, find someone else to love, get married and have a family. Time was beginning to run out. When I sat down and explained all this to Roy, he quietly took it in and made no attempt to try and change my mind. I think he knew this was coming and, after being together for nearly ten years, understood me well enough to know that once I had made up my mind I was not one for changing it. He also wanted me to achieve a lot more than just messing about on boats, and knew that I was capable of doing this. To this end, I received a lot of support and encouragement from Roy after my return to UK. No bad words were spoken, and I knew he would always remain my best friend.

Whilst I had been away Roy had picked up a couple of extra crew, which I was really pleased about. Not only was it good to share the workload between four rather than just the two of us, it also helped having company as it did detract a little from the sad moments of thinking about our impending break-up. We arrived back in dear Fort Lauderdale on 7 December. Not wanting to prolong the parting, I flew back to London a week later. I had to leave Boots behind. Apart from the cost, I just couldn't put him through six months' quarantine back in England, and in any case I had no idea where I would end up living. The boat was his home, and I know, given the choice, he would want to remain there. He must have wondered why I was making his fur all wet when we had our last cuddle. Not wanting Roy to come with me to the airport, we parted when I got on the shuttle bus. It was a little awkward as neither of us wanted to display too much emotion in front of a busload of people. To everyone else it looked like we were saying goodbye for just a short period of time. In reality, after nearly ten years, it was the final act of parting forever. I was now on my own and full of mixed emotions. Yes, I was terribly sad at leaving Roy, but a good part of me was excited. Here I was, in 1977 at the age of twenty-nine, about to start a new phase of my life, and I was ready to face whatever challenges lay ahead of me and determined to deal with them in a very positive way. Bring it on!

Epilogue

Two years later Roy married a lovely lady, Barbara, who was around the same age as him, and moved ashore, remaining in Fort Lauderdale. Barbara was a great cat lover, so Boots shared the house with two other cats. As he didn't really seem to like this arrangement too much, he took off. I would like to think he found a new, loving home, or maybe he headed back to the marina and found another boat. One thing's for sure – he was a survivor, and I feel certain he would have lived a full life.

About to board a Sea Prince for a joy ride,
Lossiemouth 1967

One of Tugg Wilson's sketches done on *Spirit of Cutty Sark*
between Malta and Gibraltar, November 1969

Promoted to Leading Wren just before
deserting in October 1969

On *Spirit of Cutty Sark*, Bequia 1970

Spirit of Cutty Sark November 1969–January 1971

Heading towards the Frangipani Hotel, Bequia 1970

Aquavit Roy, Mike White and myself. Yacht delivery, UK to California, March-September 1972

Heroism Cited
In Liner Blaze

By GORDON JOSELOFF

BRIDGETOWN, Barbados (UPI) — Passengers and crewmen of the rescue ship Queen Elizabeth II told yesterday of a night of heroism when 635 persons escaped the cruise liner Antilles ablaze from stem to stern and driven hard on an uncharted reef in the dark and choppy Caribbean.

All 635 lives were saved but the $15 million Antilles, a sleek 600-foot vessel of the French Lines, was destroyed in what a company official described as "a stunning catastrophe."

Several American passengers on the Antilles said they were unable to understand

tilles passengers appeared hurt, according to Healy.

"The rescue operation went smoothly."

The QE2 picked up 501 passengers and crew. Forty-nine others were taken in the yacht Cutty Sark to the nearby island of Bequia. Eighty-five were aboard the French Line freighter Suffern bound for Barbados.

The captain of the Antilles, Ramon Kerverdo, was among those on Bequia.

THE ANTILLES, built in 1952, was the French Lines No. 2 ship after the flagship France. It was en route to Barbados on a tour of the Caribbean that began in San Juan, Puerto Rico, on Jan. 4.

Best hire car ever! Madeira 1972

GIRL PHONES HOME
FROM WEST INDIES :
'I've lost my right foot'

A TELEPHONE call to Mr and Mrs John Pegg of 47 Woodland Way, Ongar, last Thursday from their eldest daughter Teresa in the West Indies informed them that she had lost her right foot in an accident off St Vincent.

·Teresa, 22, formerly a popular sports captain at Ongar Secondary School, was in the WRENS for nearly three years but has recently been working as a hostess on the sloop

TERESA PEGG   ★ (560)

Spirit of Cutty Sark. This vessel, which came fourth in the 1968 singlehanded trans-Atlantic race, is now used to take wealthy Americans on cruises around the islands.

As far as her mother could make out, Teresa's foot got caught in a rope on the deck.

"Not to worry, they've tidied it up" she said over the phone.

"She asked us to let our local doctor know" said Mrs Audrey Pegg. "She is now staying with an English family at St Vincent. We are all waiting to do all we can for her. . . . Her whole life has been so very active."

At school Teresa was captain of netball and while in the WRENS was often flown from Scotland to the south to take part in representative badminton matches.

In her last letter home she told how she had helped in the rescue of people from the French liner which struck a reef off St Vincent; during the Torrey Canyon oil spill she

acted as rangefinder for Buccaneer pilots who were sent to bomb the tanker.

Also working on the Spirit of Cutty Sark is Richard Thwaites of Moreton, the boyfriend of Teresa's 21-year-old sister Janet. Mr and Mrs Pegg also have another daughter, Karen, aged nine.

● A cablegram received from Teresa this week said that she would be home on Saturday.

With Julie on Young Island dock having just been discharged from St Vincent Hospital, February 1971

Wearing a tight fitting stocking over my prosthesis to help prevent chaffing to the stump

▷ A line feeding out fast under heavy tension can be most dangerous as the unfortunate Terry Pegg discovered on *Spirit of Cutty Sark*. She threw a line on to the jetty with boat moving fast away from the jetty and her foot caught in a bight of the line and was promptly torn off. This happened alongside the jetty at Mustique. A plane was at the airfield, a radio message was sent to St. Vincent to the hospital, and within an hour she was in the operating room and well taken care of by Dr. Porter Smith of *Christiana*. She is doing an amazing job of recovery, exhibiting a tremendous reserve of courage and cheerfullness, and states that she will be back on *Cutty Sark* in the near future sailing as cook hostess.

Yachting Magazine, April 1971

IN THE hot seat: an authentic fire-breathing Chinese dragon holds no fears for 'Boots', ship's cat on the Intrepid Dragon 11. Looking on are Captain Roy Williams and crew member Terry Pegg. The junk sails tomorrow or Friday.

The Royal Gazette, Bermuda 15 June 1977

Officer's Quarters, Nelson's Dockyard just before it became a museum (Hans Hoffman in foreground) Antigua Race Week April 1977

Intrepid Dragon II, February 1975-December 1977

Start of the Antigua/Guadeloupe race 1977 Ticonderoga is in the lead with me helming *Antigua* April 1977

About the Author

Now in her seventies Terri still remains very active and enjoys living life to the full. She loves playing pickleball and hopes to continue doing so for some time yet. Since her return to the UK in 1977 Terri has constantly been a volunteer for more than one organisation or charity

In 1983 Terri married Pete, and whilst living in Hong Kong their daughter Jane was born, followed by Andrew four years later back in Ascot.

Terri and Pete now live on the Surrey/Hampshire border and have a small cabin cruiser at the bottom of their garden on the Basingstoke Canal, which enables them to continue messing about on water in a very convenient way.

In between being a granny, playing pickleball and bridge, and enjoying her social life, Terri has started making notes in preparation for her next book covering her varied and interesting career years along with some personal challenges. Throughout her life she really has proven there is no such word as 'can't'. Watch this space!

ACKNOWLEDGEMENTS

I do hope you have enjoyed reading my book. Thank you for buying it, and I welcome your comments. My email address is: terriinskip48@gmail.com

I have dedicated this book to my beautiful family, in particular my wonderful husband, Pete. Without his encouragement and support, this book would have remained in one of my personal folders gathering dust.

A big thank you to Roy's wife, Barbara, who took the trouble to get the old ship's logs from Florida to me in the UK after he died in 1987. They were invaluable in jogging my memory and providing accurate information, and goodness me, they brought back so many fond memories.

Writing a book is relatively easy. Getting it published is certainly a challenge; more so for a new and unknown author. Thank you, ALLi (Alliance of Independent Authors). Without your existence I would have floundered. Your good advice steered me in the right direction. Also my appreciation to Christine Hammacott from The Art of Communication for the book cover design, which I love, and formatting my work in readiness for going to print.

And finally, a big thank you to my wonderful professional editor Nicky Taylor, who worked hard with her red ink to transform my manuscript into an acceptable state for publication. The discovery that we have quite a lot in common, including our mutual love of boats and cats, has created a lovely bond of friendship.

Printed in Great Britain
by Amazon